STUDIES IN TH

UK inflation

David Heathfield

University of Southampton

Series Editor
Bryan Hurl
Head of Economics, Harrow School

Heinemann Educational Books Ltd.
Halley Court, Jordan Hill, Oxford OX2 8EJ
OXFORD LONDON EDINBURGH MELBOURNE
MADRID ATHENS BOLOGNA PARIS SYDNEY
AUCKLAND SINGAPORE TOKYO IBADAN
NAIROBI HARARE GABORONE
PORTSMOUTH NH (USA)

© David Heathfield 1992

First published 1992

British Library Cataloguing in Publication Data

A catalogue record for this book is available from the British Library

ISBN 0 435 33014 4

Typeset and illustrated by Taurus Graphics, Abingdon, Oxon.

Printed and bound in Great Britain by Clays Ltd, St Ives plc.

Acknowledgements

The Publishers would like to thank the following for permission to reproduce copyright material:

Associated Examination Board for the questions on pp. 28, 52 and 69; John Banham for the letter on p. 60; Mel Calman for the cartoons on pp. 5 and 80, which appeared in *The Times*; Central Statistical Office for the tables on pp. 15, 18, 30, 39, 60, 75, 83 and 86, the graphs on pp. 21 and 54, the figures on p. 88, and the quote on p. 62, which appeared in the *Bank of England Quarterly Bulletin* and are reproduced with the permission of The Controller of Her Majesty's Stationery Office; the *Economist* for the quote on p. 89; the *Financial Times* for the extract on p. 61; Wynne Godley for the letters on pp. 37 and 43; Charles Hanson for the letter on p. 16; International Monetary Fund for the table on p. 4 which appeared in *International Financial Statistics*; the *Independent* for the extract on p. 43; the *Independent on Sunday* for the extract on p. 41; Joint Matriculation Board for the questions on pp. 9, 59 and 82; Richard Layard for the letter on p. 61; Stephen Lewis for the extract on p. 41; Oxford and Cambridge Schools Examinations Board for the questions on pp. 9, 20–21, 29, 38, 53 and 82; Professor W Parker for the question on p. 9; Reuters for the extract on p. 8; Nicholas Ridley for the letter on p. 37; Southern Universities Joint Board for the question on p. 82; *The Times* for the extracts on pp. 2, 8, 16, 18, 37 and 60, and the illustrations on pp. 5 and 80; *Today* for the extract on p. 87; University of Cambridge Local Examinations Syndicate for the questions on pp. 28, 38 and 53; University of London School Examinations Board for the questions on pp. 29, 38, 53, 59 and 82; University of Oxford Delegacy of Local Examinations for the questions on pp. 29, 39, 53 and 82; Peter Warburton for the letter on p. 43; Welsh Joint Education Committee for the question on p. 53.

The Publishers have made every attempt to contact the correct copyright holders. If, however, any material has been incorrectly attributed, the Publishers would be happy to correct this at the earliest opportunity.

Contents

Preface and Acknowledgement		*iv*
Chapter One	Defining inflation	1
Chapter Two	Measuring inflation	10
Chapter Three	Costs and benefits of inflation	22
Chapter Four	Monetarist explanations	32
Chapter Five	The Keynesian view	40
Chapter Six	Cost-push inflation	55
Chapter Seven	Expectations	62
Chapter Eight	Economic policies	70
Chapter Nine	Conclusions	84
Index		90

Preface

The conquest of inflation seems to rule unchallenged as the primary policy goal of UK governments. Futhermore, according to the Chancellor of the Exchequer, 'being jobless is a price worth paying to beat inflation'.

This study by David Heathfield covers the problems of which definitions to use for the measurement of inflation, the micro and macro gains and losses for economic agents, and the conflict over which policy instruments to use to contain it. Additionally – and not before time – rational expectations feature, but in a form that is, at last, intelligible to both teachers and taught!

The study of inflation is a core part of A and AS syllabuses in Economics. The examination boards' essay and data response questions in each chapter measure how far David Heathfield has succeeded in his aim.

Bryan Hurl
Series Editor

Acknowledgement

Since first agreeing to write this volume in Studies in the UK Economy, I have been in frequent contact with the series editor, Bryan Hurl. Bryan has provided an enormous amount of help, advice and encouragement. The arrangement of material and the style of presentation owe much to his detailed comments. It would be inappropriate to publish it under my name without this acknowledgement.

DFH, Southampton, November 1991

Chapter One
Defining inflation

' *"When I use a word,"* Humpty Dumpty said, *"it means just what I want it to mean."* ' Lewis Carroll, *Alice Through the Looking Glass*

What is being inflated?
It is difficult to trace the time when the word '**inflation**' began to take on its modern meaning. In everyday parlance, to 'inflate' something is to fill it with gas so that it swells up. When we have economic inflation what is being swollen is usually **price level**; but some commentators mean that it is money supply that is being inflated, and possibly price level changes because of that. Early economic textbooks rarely used the word inflation in the technical sense used here, but spoke instead of inflating the money supply or the quantity of credit in the economy. This inflation of money supply, or credit, is an increase 'beyond what is merited' and is associated with (is deemed to cause) increases in the general price level.

Today there can be little doubt that inflation means a *sustained increase in the aggregate price level* and has replaced unemployment and growth at the top of the political agenda. Indeed, judging from the stream of comments from politicians, journalists and business people, the control of inflation is not only more important than, it is a necessary precondition for, full employment and for sustainable economic growth. We shall explore later the strengths of these claims. For the moment it is sufficient to note that much of our national economic life is dominated by the widely perceived need to control inflation: see, for example, the extract from *The Times* reproduced on page 2.

In this chapter we shall examine in more detail what is meant by inflation. First we look at the role of the **price mechanism** and how it provides the necessary ingredients for inflation to come about.

The price mechanism
One of the major contributions made by economists to an understanding of the workings of our society is the analysis of the price mechanism. Largely as a result of the work of Adam Smith, we have come to

UK inflation

We have licked inflation, says buoyant Major
© Times Newspapers Ltd, 1991

Britain's inflation rate fell to 4.7 per cent in August, the lowest level for more than three years, prompting renewed speculation of a further cut in interest rates and an early general election.

The fall from 5.5 per cent in July was slightly less than the City had expected, but enough to inspire John Major to declare that inflation had been licked.

The figures also suggest that the headline rate might drop to the Chancellor's 4 per cent target or less when the next retail prices index is published on October 11 – just as the prime minister rises to address the last day of the Conservative party conference. The City and West-minster believe he may use that occasion to cut interest rates and call an election for November 7.

Yesterday Mr Major welcomed the August figures, saying: "We can be confident now that we have got inflation licked in a way we have not seen for many years." Norman Lamont noted that Britain's inflation rate was now below the European Community average and would soon fall to levels comparable with the best in Europe.

The Times, 14 September 1991

see that if individual economic agents (workers, landowners, shoppers, investors etc.) buy at the lowest prices and sell at the highest prices then both they, as individuals, and society as a whole will be as well off as it is possible to be (in a material sense).

When there are shortages sellers raise prices, and this encourages suppliers to supply more and encourages buyers to look for alternative goods. When there are surpluses prices fall, which discourages suppliers and encourages buyers. Figures 1 and 2 show the effects on prices

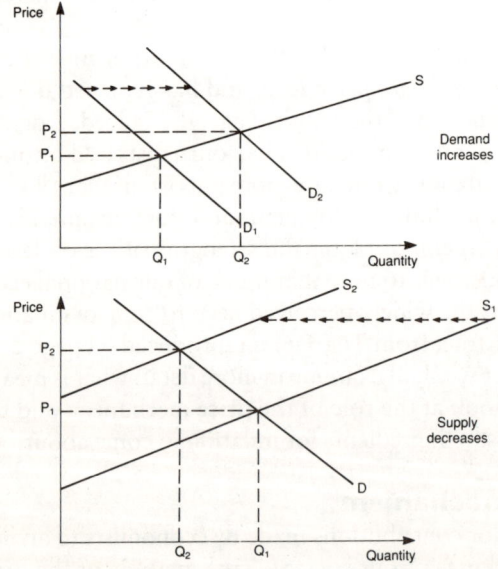

Figure 1 Illustrating the price mechanism

Defining inflation

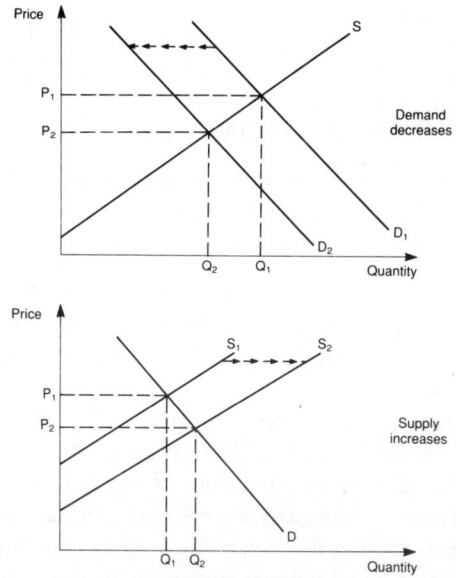

Figure 2 Illustrating the price mechanism

and quantities of:

- an increase in demand from D_1 to D_2 with no change in the position of the supply curve;
- a decrease in supply from S_1 to S_2 with no change in the position of the demand curve;
- a decrease in demand from D_1 to D_2 with no change in the position of the supply curve; and
- an increase in supply from S_1 to S_2 with no change in the position of the demand curve.

What this demonstrates is that *flexible prices are necessary for markets to work efficiently*. Price fluctuations will signal to suppliers and to demanders where there are shortages and where there are surpluses.

Communism, perestroika and inflation

Some economic systems have tried to do without the free price mechanism and have relied instead on central planners to fix prices and to determine what will be produced and for whom. Rationing – the allocation of scarce resources – is done by *queuing* rather than by price rises, and those who are willing and able to spend hours queuing get the goods.

UK inflation

Queuing is clearly a huge waste of time and not the most efficient way of allocating resources, but queuing for goods was largely the case in communist countries under central planning. But with *perestroika*, Mr Gorbachev extolled the efficacy of the price mechanism:

'It is only with the market that you can realize the principle of distribution according to labour. That means that socialism and the market are not just compatible, but essentially inseparable'.

Once the market is allowed to work again it is no longer possible for central planners to fix prices and generate queues. Shortages will cause prices to rise and hence inflation is likely to emerge when the controls are taken off.

However, the reappearance of inflation in centrally planned economies has varied considerably and has not necessarily been associated with the degree of partial administrative de-centralization since 1970. Table 1 shows some consumer price changes in Eastern Europe between 1971 and 1989. Some of these countries have by and large adhered to a fixed-price regime of orthodox central planning. Price changes have been slow and spread over many years. Hungary and Poland have experienced some upward drift since the mid–70s, with Poland really taking off in the 1980s. The Soviet Union, Bulgaria, Czechoslovakia and East Germany kept prices fairly constant for a long time and have, apart from one or two blips, only very recently experienced anything like inflation. These blips do, however, signify that inflation can occur in centrally planned economies long before any liberalization could have been envisaged.

Table 1 Consumer price developments in Eastern Europe and the Soviet Union, 1971–89 (previous year = 100)

	1971–1975	1976–1980	1981–1985	1985	1986	1987	1988	1989
Bulgaria	0.9	20.7	4.5	1.7	3.5	0.1	−1.3	9.2
Czechoslovakia	0.4	10.2	8.9	1.3	0.5	0.1	0.2	1.4
East Germany	−1.1	0.5	0.3	−0.1	0.0	0.0	0.0	2.0
Hungary	13.7	31.5	34.1	7.0	4.5	8.0	16.5	18.0
Poland	12.2	34.1	179.1	14.4	17.7	23.5	60.0	244.1
Romania	2.6	7.4	25.0	−0.4	−0.1	0.2	..	..
USSR	0.0	4.2	5.5	2.0	2.0	1.0	0.4	2.3

Sources: Various national statistics and the IMF's *International Financial Statistics*; some figures are estimates

Defining inflation

In a dynamic, ever-changing, free-market economy we would expect prices to be always on the move – some going up and some going down and perhaps a few remaining the same. This is indeed our common experience. The price of fresh flowers on Mothering Sunday is two or three times higher than on the following day. Supermarkets cover their windows with information about price reductions and invite us to buy 'while prices are low'.

It is not absolutely necessary for some prices to fall in order for the price mechanism to work. Buyers can be persuaded to buy less bread and more potatoes simply by increasing the price of bread *relative* to the price of potatoes. Similarly producers can be persuaded to produce fewer potatoes and more bread by increasing the price of bread *relative* to the price of potatoes. Thus if both prices rose but bread price rose more than potato price, then the **relative price change** would be sufficient for the price mechanism to work.

For the shopper the question to be asked is this. If some prices are rising and some prices are falling *relative* to each other, will it be the case that there will be sufficient price falls to offset the price rises? That is, what is happening to prices in general?

It is this question – what is happening to prices on average? – that concerns us. Relative prices must, and do, change but relative prices are not our concern. We are here concerned only with their aggregate (average) behaviour.

Purchasing power

Most commentators believe that in the best of all possible worlds there would be no change in the general level of prices. Relative prices would be adjusted in such a way that each price rise would be exactly balanced by a price fall elsewhere. The general level of prices may fluctuate over time simply because it is rarely possible to arrange for the individual price rises and falls to coincide. Sometimes there will be more falls than rises and at other times there will be more rises than falls. Thus average price level will fluctuate, but these fluctuations should even out over time so that there is no long-run tendency for the general level of price to rise or fall.

What almost everyone wants to avoid is a sustained rise in the general level of prices. This *sustained (secular) rise in the general level of prices* is what is meant by the word 'inflation'.

To see what inflation means for those on fixed incomes, consider households with £100 to spend every week. They have to decide each week which are the best buys to put in their baskets. As relative prices change, the best buys change too, so goods whose prices have fallen are substituted for those whose prices have risen; but, on balance, with no inflation, the shoppers are equally well off every week.

If, however, there is inflation (i.e. price rises are not compensated for by price falls elsewhere) then the shoppers become progressively worse off. As time goes by the £100 buys fewer goods.

This gives us another way of defining inflation – it is the *secular decline in the purchasing power of money*. With each successive year the pound is worth less in terms of the goods it can buy, and so inflation can be seen as a secular erosion of the value of the currency.

Table 2 shows how the value of the pound sterling – in terms of its ability to be exchanged for goods in the UK – has changed between 1920 and 1990.

Table 2 Purchasing power of the pound

1920	1925	1930	1935	1940	1945	1950	1955
100	125	135	157	129	111	98	76
1960	1965	1970	1975	1980	1985	1990	
66	56	46	27	13	8.9	6.8	

Reading along the rows we see that £100 in 1920 increased in value until 1935, when you could buy half as much again for your £100 – i.e. £157-worth of 1920 goods. Average price level had therefore been falling over that period. Since 1935, however, the pound has lost value. By 1950 we had returned to the same purchasing power as we had in 1920, and by 1990 the pound would buy only 6.8p-worth of 1920 goods! Someone who put his savings under his mattress in 1920 would have lost about 93 per cent of its value seventy years later.

Pure inflation

Of course, inflation can occur even when there are no changes in relative prices. If the price of every good were to double, then *relative* prices would remain unchanged but the *aggregate* price level would double. The shopper would find that £100 would buy only half the quantity of goods and there would be no price incentive to switch from some goods to others. Inflation of this kind (let us call it **pure inflation**) has no role to play in the efficient operation of the price mechanism since there are no changes in relative prices to reflect relative shortages (or surpluses).

In the case of pure inflation it is easy to see that a doubling of price level will halve the purchasing power of money – the purchasing power of money is therefore the *reciprocal* of the change in the price level. In this particular case the price level doubled (×2) and purchasing power halved (×½), but the same holds for a 10 per cent increase in price level. If price rises by 10 per cent (×1.1) the purchasing power falls by slightly more than 9 per cent (×1/1.1 = 0.90909).

The rate of inflation

Until now we have considered increases in price level but have said nothing about how long it takes for these changes to come about. In what follows we shall be considering the rate of change of price level – the **rate of inflation**. Typically we shall be comparing the price level at one point of time with the price level one year later. This is what is meant by the **year-on-year figure** and it measures the annual rate of inflation for a particular twelve-month period.

If price level doubled in one year then the annual rate of inflation would be 100 per cent, but if this doubling of price level took 22 years then the annual rate of inflation would be only 2 per cent. It is the *rate* of change of price level which is of interest rather than the *absolute* change in price level. Few shoppers would be too concerned at an annual rate of inflation of only 2 per cent but many would look askance at 100 per cent in a year.

Degrees of inflation

Aldcroft (1990) suggests that four degrees of inflation can be helpfully, if somewhat arbitrarily, distinguished. First there is **creeping inflation** which is persistent but at a low level – less than 10 per cent. Second comes **severe inflation** which occurs at rates between 10 and 100 per cent. Third is **galloping inflation**, at between 100 and 1000 per cent.

Finally there is **hyperinflation** (greater than 1000 per cent a year) which gets so high as to lead to the destruction of the currency.

Hyperinflation
When there is hyperinflation the currency can be used neither as a medium of exchange nor as a store of value. The rate at which money is losing its purchasing power is so rapid that between receiving wages and spending them they will have lost an appreciable amount of their value. No-one therefore wants to hold or use money. This applies equally to those who are selling and those who are buying. Shop–

keepers are reluctant to sell (exchange their goods for money) when the value of the money is falling all the time.

> # Argentine prices double in days
>
> **Buenos Aires (Reuter)** – Supermarkets and stores remained closed yesterday even though the Government unveiled economic measures aimed at halting the hyperinflation crippling the Argentine economy for the second time in six months. Business came to a virtual standstill as a bank holiday lengthened a hectic new year weekend during which some consumer prices more than doubled.
>
> Shops in poor areas of the capital shut down.
>
> Señor Daniel Mon, a shopkeeper in Buenos Aires, said: "We lost money on everything we sold on Saturday because prices have risen between 100 and 200 per cent. Some of us prefer to wait until the dust settles instead of losing more money."
>
> - **Lima**: Official figures released yesterday show that prices in Peru rose 33.8 per cent in December, bringing the 1989 inflation rate to 2775.3 per cent.
>
> 3.1.90
>
> © Times Newspapers Ltd., 1990

Hyperinflations were few and far between before the turn of this century – although the French Revolution did result in an eighteen-fold increase in price level between 1795 and 1796, and during the American Civil War the price level in the Confederacy rose from 1 to 12 between 1863 and 1865.

These may seem bad enough but are nothing compared with what has happened in this century. After the First World War hyperinflations occurred in Austria, Germany, Hungary, Poland and Russia. These resulted in increases in the price level ranging from 100 *billion* per cent in Germany (the highest) to 4400 per cent in Hungary (the lowest).

Things were even worse after the Second World War, affecting China, Greece and Hungary. The worst case was that of Hungary where inflation reached its peak of 42 000 thousand billion per cent in July 1946. This resulted in an increase in price level in Hungary of 3.8 per cent with 27 noughts on the end, and in China of 1 billion per cent.

It is the experience of hyperinflation and its destruction of currencies – particularly in Europe in the first half of this century – which lies at the root of many people's terror of inflation. To them, inflation of any kind will tend to lead to hyperinflation and hyperinflation must be avoided at all costs. We look at this again later.

In the UK and in most developed countries it is clear that:

- There have been fluctuations in the rate of inflation, but all changes are positive so that the price level continues to rise – albeit at an uneven rate.
- All countries have experienced inflation.
- There is a very wide variation in rates of inflation among countries.

The phenomenon of inflation is therefore widespread, uneven, feared and in need of explanation.

KEY WORDS

Inflation	Rate of inflation
Price level	Year-on-year figure
Price mechanism	Creeping inflation
Relative price change	Severe inflation
Purchasing power	Galloping inflation
Pure inflation	Hyperinflation

Reading list
Aldcroft, D., 'Inflation in the twentieth century', *Economic Review*, Jan. 1990.
Dictionary of Modern Economics, Penguin.
Heathfield, D. and Russell, Chapter 16 in *Modern Economics*, 2nd edn, Simon & Schuster, 1991.
Maunder, P., Myers, D., Wall, N., and LeRoy Miller, Chapters 11 and 30 in *Economics Explained: A Coursebook in A-Level Economics*, 2nd edn, Collins Educational, 1991.

Essay topics
1. Define inflation and explain why it is widely regarded as a problem. Does the current rate of 5 per cent mean that the control of inflation is no longer a problem? (Joint Matriculation Board, 1988).
2. 'Economic history forms one leg of the chair on which an educated economist must sit to do useful work' (Prof. W.N. Parker). Explain, with examples from your own studies, how economic history can help in the understanding of contemporary economics. (Oxford & Cambridge Schools Examination Board, 1987)

Chapter Two
Measuring inflation

'There are lies, damned lies and statistics.'   Disraeli

Introduction
To measure the annual rate of change of price we have to measure the price level at one point in time and measure it again twelve months later. A kilogramme of sugar, for example, may sell for £1.50 on 1 January 1991 and for £2.00 on 1 January 1992. The increase in price is therefore easily measured as £0.50 over the twelve-month period. The *annual rate of change* of sugar price will then be 0.5/1.5 = 0.3333 = 33 per cent.

If we know that the prices of all goods have risen by the same proportionate amount, as would be the case with pure inflation, then a 33 per cent increase in the price of one good means a 33 per cent increase in the price of all goods. Thus by measuring the annual increase in the price of any one good we have the annual rate of inflation.

Unfortunately there is rarely, if ever, an occurrence of pure inflation. Typically some prices rise a lot, others rise only a little, some remain unchanged and still others fall. The problem then is to measure the 'aggregate' price when there is no common behaviour among individual prices.

There is no ideal solution to this question but there are plenty of second best solutions.

Choosing a representative basket
Consider for the moment a rather simple economy in which there are only four goods – say bread, tea, cloth and coal. Each has its price in pounds so that, for example, bread costs £0.50 per kilo, tea £2.50 per litre, cloth £5.00 per square metre and coal £2.00 per kilo. Twelve months later the price of bread has increased by 100 per cent to £1.00 per kilo, that of tea has fallen by 20 per cent to £2.00 per litre, that of cloth has remained unchanged and that of coal has risen by 50 per cent to £3.00 per kilo.

Relative prices have clearly changed and there is no single good which can be taken as representative of goods in general. It is therefore necessary to find some way of combining the four price changes to yield a 'representative' aggregate price change.

Measuring inflation

The most obvious way of doing this is to choose a particular combination of goods and calculate the price (value) of that combination. The price so found is then compared with the price of the same combination of goods one year later.

To see how this works, consider a combination (or 'basket') of goods comprising one kilo of bread, one litre of tea, one square metre of cloth and one kilo of coal. To buy this **basket of goods** at their original prices would cost £10.00, which is therefore the 'price' of the basket. One year later that *same* basket of goods would cost £11.00. The aggregate price – the price of the basket of goods – has therefore risen by £1.00, or 10 per cent of the original. All this is summarized in Table 3.

Table 3

	Quantity	First price	Second price	First value	Second value	Change value	Change (%)
Bread	1 kilo	£0.50	£1.00	£0.50	£1.00	+£0.50	+100
Tea	1 litre	£2.50	£2.00	£2.50	£2.00	−£0.50	−20
Cloth	1 metre	£5.00	£5.00	£5.00	£5.00	£0.00	0
Coal	1 kilo	£2.00	£3.00	£2.00	£3.00	+£1.00	+50
Totals				£10.00	£11.00	£1.00	**10**

This is clearly one way of generating a measure of aggregate price change (inflation rate) but it is not entirely satisfactory. To start with, the measure of inflation rate depends on what combination of goods is chosen. We can illustrate this quite well by applying the same price changes to a different basket of the same goods. If, for example, we choose a basket comprising one kilo of bread, 20 litres of tea, one square metre of cloth and 0.5 kilos of coal, the price of this basket at the *original set of prices* would be:

$$1 \times £0.50 + 20 \times £2.50 + 1 \times £5.00 + 0.5 \times £2.00 = £56.50$$

The price of the same basket twelve months later would be:

$$1 \times £1.00 + 20 \times £2.00 + 1 \times £5.00 + 0.5 \times £3.00 = £47.50$$

This is summarised in Table 4.

Thus, by changing the contents of the basket, it is possible to change an increase in aggregate price of 10 per cent to a *decrease* in aggregate price of 16 per cent!

It is easy to see from the tables that the percentage changes in individual prices are the same but the percentage change in the aggregate price – the price of the basket – is quite different between the two tables.

Obviously the increase in the quantity of tea, the price of which fell, increases the influence of the price fall on the value of the whole basket. Had we increased the quantity of coal then the value of the basket would have increased when the prices changed, and would have increased considerably.

Table 4

	Quantity	First price	Second price	First value	Second value	Change value	Change (%)
Bread	1 kilo	£0.50	£1.00	£0.50	£1.00	+£0.50	+100
Tea	20 litre	£2.50	£2.00	£50.00	£40.00	−£10.00	−20
Cloth	1 metre	£5.00	£5.00	£5.00	£5.00	£0.00	0
Coal	0.5 kilo	£2.00	£3.00	£1.00	£1.50	+£0.50	+50
Totals				£56.50	£47.50	−£9.00	−16

The choice of basket is therefore crucial. Unfortunately there is no single basket which can be ranked above all others as yielding the 'best' measure of inflation, and we are reduced to choosing whichever basket best serves our immediate needs.

Cost of living index

One of the earliest attempts at measuring aggregate price changes in the UK was begun in 1914 with the object of measuring the **cost of living** of working-class families. That is to say, there was an interest in finding out by how much wages should be changed in order to allow workers to maintain their standard of living when prices were changing. If aggregate price level rose by 10 per cent, then the cost of living rose by 10 per cent so wages should rise by 10 per cent too. The appropriate basket of goods for such a purpose is that representing the purchases typically made by working-class families and, at that time, included basic items such as bread, potatoes and candles.

Retail price index

In 1947, after the Second World War, the official cost of living index was replaced by a more comprehensive measure of aggregate price change – the **retail price index**. The RPI has become the basic measure of domestic inflation in the UK.

In order to compute this price index the government set out to discover the expenditure pattern of a typical UK household via a large-scale *Household Expenditure Survey*. A sample of households throughout the UK were asked to report on how they spent their incomes, and from this information a typical basket was formed. Since 1957 there has been an annual survey of some 7000 households (the *Family Expenditure Survey* or FES), and these surveys provide the basis for the basket underlying the RPI. These 7000 households exclude pensioner households and the very rich households; by 'pensioner household' is meant households in which three-quarters of the income comes from pensions, and by 'very rich' is meant the top 3–4 per cent of earners. The expenditure pattern of the typical households determines the basket of goods for the RPI.

The expenditure pattern is of course changing all the time. We no longer rely on candles to light our houses and offices, and rarely burn coal to heat them. We do, however, buy video recorders and compact discs which simply were not available when the index was started. The appropriate basket is therefore continually changing and we are faced with the problem of deciding which basket to use.

The solution is to keep the basket fixed for a year at a time but to revise the basket every year in line with changes in the pattern of expenditure. Thus the FES has to be carried out every year. The basket for 1991 comprised some 600 separate indicators and is shown in Figure 3. It is clear that our greatest expenditure is on housing and household goods, and this is followed by travel and leisure and then by food and catering.

If our total expenditure – the whole basket – is given the value of 1000 points, then expenditure on housing and household goods would constitute 353 points, travel and leisure would be 239 points, food and catering 198 points, alcohol and tobacco 109 points and personal expenditure 101 points. These 'points' represent the relative importance of these items in consumers' expenditure and are called **weights**. The areas devoted to each item in the pie-chart reflect these weights, so that 'housing and household expenditure' is about three times as big as 'personal expenditure'. The larger the weight the bigger the influence it has on the RPI. Thus if the price of 'housing and household expenditure' (353 points) rose by 10 per cent it would have three times the effect on the RPI as would a 10 per cent rise in the price of 'personal expenditure' (101 points).

Now we have the basket for 1991 we need information on the price changes of each of its elements. The RPI is intended to be a measure of how much aggregate price level has *changed* rather than a measure of the *level* of aggregate prices. Every month 100 000 price movements of some 600 types of goods and services are monitored and combined into a single figure using the weights of the basket. These month-on-month changes in the aggregate price are the RPI.

The RPI therefore measures the monthly change in the value of a basket of consumer goods. The basket represents the expenditure pattern

UK inflation

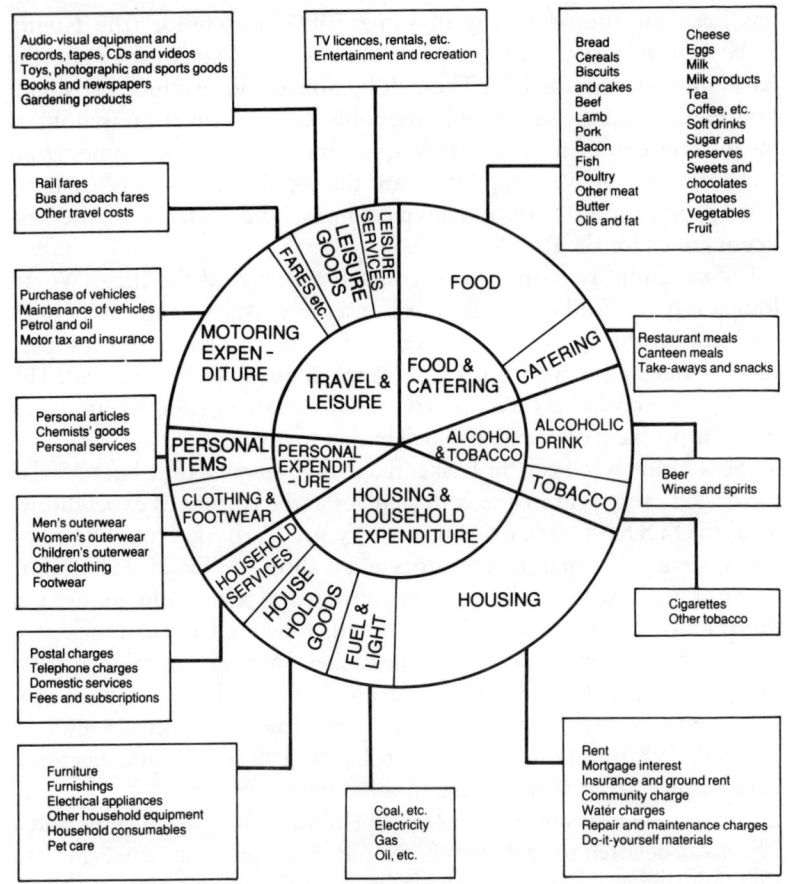

Figure 3 Structure of the RPI in 1991

of a typical household and is updated every year to reflect the changing expenditure patterns over time.

These month-on-month changes can be linked together to provide comparisons of aggregate price levels between years, and Figure 4 shows how the RPI has behaved between 1971 and 1991. It will be evident from this figure that inflation – the rate of change of aggregate price level – has varied quite a lot, with the highest rate being over 25 per cent a year and the lowest being less than 5 per cent a year. The aggregate price level never fell (or even remained constant) during those 20 years.

Table 5 shows how the aggregate price level has changed since 1962 compared with that in January 1974. This is found by adding the annual changes and taking the level in January 1974 to be 100.

Measuring inflation

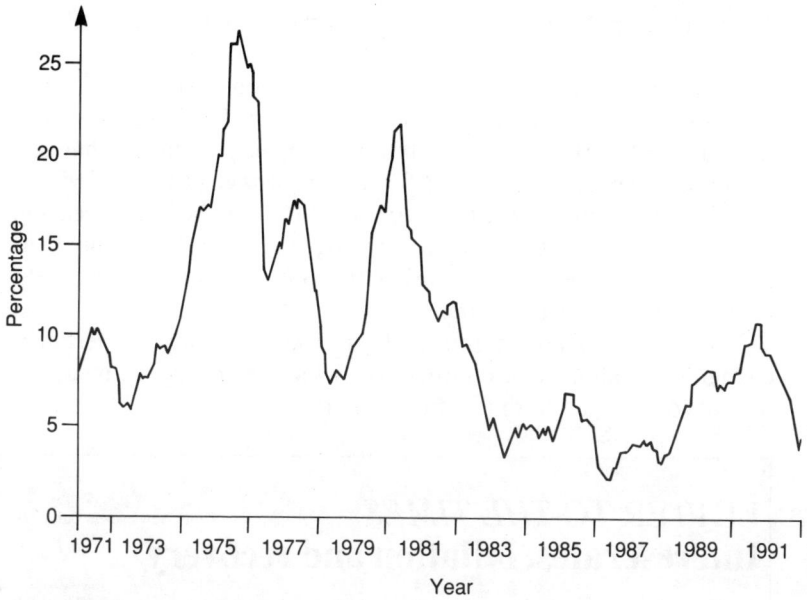

Figure 4 RPI 1971–1991

Table 5 Movement of aggregate price level in UK, 1962 to 1991

1962	1970	1971	1972	1973	1974	1975	1976
53.0	73.1	80.0	85.7	93.5	108.5	134.8	157.1

1977	1978	1979	1980	1981	1982	1983	1984
182.0	197.1	223.5	263.7	295.0	320.4	335.1	351.8

1985	1986	1987	1988	1989	1990	1991	
373.2	385.9	402.0	421.7	454.5	497.5	525.1 (to April)	

Table 6 Change of price index from January 1990 (=100) to March 1991

Jan	Feb	Mar	Apr	May	Jun	Jul	Aug
100.0	100.6	101.6	104.7	105.6	106.0	106.1	107.2

Sep	Oct	Nov	Dec	Jan	Feb	Mar	
108.2	109.0	108.7	108.7	108.9	109.5	110.0	

Source: *Monthly Digest of Statistics*, May 1991

The monthly figures for 1990 and early 1991 in Table 6 show that over that period the price index rose steadily from 100.0 in January to

109.0 in October. It then fell slightly over the two remaining months of 1990 to 108.7, before rising again in the first months of 1991. These monthly figures allow us to compute the year-on-year inflation rates. For example, from February 1990 to February 1991 the index rose from 100.6 to 109.5, so the February year-on-year index change is therefore 8.9 points, or about 8.8 per cent. Between March 1990 and March 1991 the index rose from 101.6 to 110.0, so the March year-on-year index change is therefore 8.4 points, or about 8.3 per cent. Thus, comparing the index in one month with that twelve months later yields the year-on-year inflation rate.

Choosing a different month to begin the twelve-month period or changing the number of months over which the change is measured will, of course, alter our measure of inflation.

LETTER TO *THE TIMES* © Times Newspapers Ltd, 1991
Interest rates, inflation and recovery

Sir: In the debate about the level of interest rate in the UK, little has been said about the way in which our rate of inflation is measured. On 16 February it was reported that the current rate of inflation had fallen to 9 per cent, and in comparison with that figure a base rate of interest of 13 per cent does not seem unduly high.

However, it should be remembered that this inflation rate is a purely historical figure over the period January 1990 to January 1991, and in fact since mid-October last the rate has been zero, as the retail price index shows:

1990	October	130.3
	November	130.0
	December	129.9
1991	January	130.2

Against this recent rate of zero inflation, it might be thought that a base rate of 13 per cent is somewhat excessive.

Perhaps the Chancellor of the Exchequer would tell us why he focuses exclusively on the 12-month inflation rate instead of the three-month or six-month rate. It was Harold Macmillan who stated about 30 years ago that policies were too often made on the basis of last year's Bradshaw. Isn't it time that Mr Lamont and his officials used up-to-date figures for their policy-making instead of inflicting further needless misery on the economy?

Yours faithfully,
CHARLES HANSON
Department of Economics
University of Newcastle upon Tyne
1 March 1991

The annual figures shown in Table 5 indicate that in this 30-year period the 'cost of living' rose tenfold. What could be bought for 53p in 1962 would cost £1.00 in January 1974 and £5.25 in 1991! Another way of putting this is to say that the *'internal purchasing power of the pound'* has fallen. In fact, by 1991 it had fallen to a mere 10 per cent of its 1962 value. The internal purchasing power is calculated simply by taking the inverse of the RPI. It is called the 'internal' purchasing power because it shows what a pound would buy in the UK – it is not an indication of the purchasing power of the pound abroad.

The RPI in action

One practical role for the measure of inflation is to compensate pensioners (and others on a 'fixed' income) for any general increases in prices; i.e. to compensate them for increases in the *cost of living*. Thus if the price level increases by 10 per cent, the cost of living increases by the same percentage and so pensions must be increased by 10 per cent to allow pensioners to buy the same basket of goods as they bought last year. This is what is meant by the **indexation** of pensions – they are increased every year by the amount by which the price index (the cost of living increase) has risen.

Another role for the measure of inflation is to guide wage negotiators so that wage rates can keep up with any increases in price level. There is, of course, a major difference between pensioners and wage earners. State pensioners usually pay no income tax, nor do they pay National Insurance contributions, and so their pension is their 'take home' income. Wage earners, on the other hand, typically pay income tax and National Insurance contributions on what they earn, and this drives a wedge between what they earn and their 'take home pay'. Thus if the government were to increase indirect taxes (value added tax) and reduce direct taxes (income tax), wage earners would face an increase in the prices they payed but they would also enjoy an increase in their 'take home pay' by way of compensation. The government therefore argues that basing wage settlements on an index of price level alone will lead to mistaken wage increases. Because of this the government has published an index reflecting changes in the purchasing power of 'take home' pay. This index will increase when retail prices increase and will decrease when the rate of income tax is decreased. It is called the **taxes and prices index** (TPI) and is shown in Table 7.

Recall that inflation is defined as the *secular* rise in the general price level. This has led some commentators to argue that the effects of changing community charge/rates and interest rates should be excluded from the index since they are once-for-all effects which distort the real (secular) inflation rate. The adjusted index is shown in Table 7.

This desire to exclude certain items from the index extends much further than excluding community charge and interest rates. Some economists argue that the retail price index will be erroneous because it reflects changes in VAT and petrol prices etc. These are determined by the government and OPEC and will be sharply changed from time to time according to circumstances and policies. Rarely will there be a secular rise in any of these prices, and hence their influence on the retail price index should be excluded from any measure of the '*sustained* rise in the general price level'.

UK inflation

Table 7 RPI, TPI and 'RPI less rates etc.'

Year	RPI	TPI	RPI less rates etc.
1978	100.0	100.0	100.0
1979	109.3	106.1	108.6
1980	129.4	123.2	127.3
1981	146.3	140.4	141.3
1982	163.9	162.3	159.3
1983	172.0	170.7	169.1
1984	180.8	177.9	176.6
1985	189.9	184.7	184.6
1986	200.4	192.9	193.2
1987	208.2	198.0	199.6
1988	215.0	N/A	206.6
1989	231.1	212.1	217.8
1990	248.8	225.5	230.5
1991	271.0	244.7	247.7

All figures relate to the month of January
Source: *Monthly Digest of Statistics*, May 1991

An index which excludes mortgage interest rate, poll tax and petrol prices is published. Since it is supposed to truly reflect inflation rate, it is called the core inflation rate or the **underlying inflation** rate. To save any possible confusion, the full retail price index is referred to as the **headline figure**.

LEADER, *THE TIMES*, 30 MARCH 1991
Measuring prices

Next week most prices in Britain will rise by 2.5 per cent, reflecting the new VAT rate which comes into effect on Monday. *As a result, inflation will fall.* This prediction can be made with absolute confidence, for April's retail price index will be determined not by retail prices but by mortgage rates and poll tax. As a result, the confusion about Britain's true inflation performance will continue, even as RPI figures improve.

Last year, John Major, as Chancellor, waxed eloquent about the way Britain's inflation rate was exaggerated by rising mortgage interest rates – a 'price' which arguably reflected the cost of capital, not the cost of living, and which other European countries excluded from their versions of the RPI. This introduced a perversity into economic policymaking in Britain: the high interest rates which were designed to control inflation actually made it worse. The switch from rates to poll tax added another perversity of the same kind. Designed to combat inflation by making local authority overspending more visible, the poll tax only added to inflationary fire.

The poll tax is mercifully headed for euthanasia but the aberrant treatment of housing costs and interest rates in Britain's RPI remains a pressing problem. Unfortunately, it is unlikely to be addressed in the short term. For what was an embarrassment for the government on the way up has become a boon on the way down. With interest rates falling and VAT-burdened consumers picking up one-third of the cost of poll tax, the much maligned headline inflation figure will soon look flatteringly subdued. This is why the government can predict with confidence that inflation will be down to 4 per cent by the winter – and why reform of the RPI if out of the question until this inflation cycle is complete.

© Times Newspapers Ltd, 1991

Other index measures

In addition to the RPI and the TPI there is a case for measuring inflation according to the price level faced by those who produce and sell UK goods and services – i.e. *the factory-gate price index*. There are two major differences between the RPI and the factory-gate price index. First, the combination of goods produced in the UK differs from the combination bought by consumers in the UK. Some goods are produced in the UK but exported to foreigners and would be excluded from the RPI, while other goods are produced in the UK but bought by UK industry (machines) or government (weapons) rather than consumers. Some goods consumed by UK consumers are imported from abroad and so are not affected by changes in UK producer prices.

Second, the factory-gate price index would use different prices. The prices received by producers differ from the prices paid by consumers by the various taxes imposed between the factory gate and the shop counter. These may be value added tax or customs and excise duties, both of which are collected by the government's collector of taxes.

The price index constructed using factory-gate prices and production quantities is called the **wholesale price index** or the 'index of producer prices'.

There are also, of course, the price levels of those goods *purchased* by UK producers (i.e. materials and fuel), and these too have an index constructed for them.

Apart from the need to compensate workers and pensioners for the consequent decreases in the real value of their incomes, the choice of inflation index depends on which gives the best account of our economic performance. The RPI clearly is a good indicator of how inflation is affecting consumers, but the producers' *output* price index is the best indicator of UK production costs and hence of our international price competitiveness. Finally, the producers' *input* price index provides an early indication of increases in producers' output prices.

There are many, many tasks for which measures of inflation and costs of living are needed and many arguments about how best to measure inflation; hence there could be any number of measures of inflation. We have looked at some of them.

Apart from the 'basket' method of measuring how aggregate price level has changed, there is another route. The Central Statistical Office (CSO) measures consumers' expenditure (*in toto*) in both current prices and in constant prices (e.g. at current prices and 1980 prices). Thus by dividing the current-priced value by the constant-priced value we can get a measure of the change in the aggregate price level. This measure is called the **consumers' expenditure deflator**. It is the index by which consumers' expenditure at current prices has to be 'deflated' to arrive at consumers' expenditure at constant (1980) prices. It will differ from the RPI insofar as it includes all the expenditure by households rather than that of a 'typical' household. Thus the expenditures by the very rich and the very poor are included.

As can be imagined there is much political interest in the construction and composition of these index numbers, and political parties tend to quote headline or core (underlying) inflation measures depending on which best supports their view of the world.

KEY WORDS

Basket of goods	Core inflation
Cost of living	Underlying inflation
Retail price index	Headline figure
Weights	Wholesale price index
Indexation	Consumers' expenditure deflator
Taxes and prices index	

Further reading

Anderton, Unit 92 in *Economics*, Causeway Press, 1991.

Chalkley, M., 'Inflation and the cost of living, *Economic Review*, May 1991.

Craven, B.M. and Gausden, R., 'How best to measure inflation?, *Royal Bank of Scotland Review*, no. 170, June 1991.

Economic Review: Data Supplement (annual).

'Measuring inflation', in *Economic Briefing No. 1*, The Treasury, Dec. 1990.

Paisley, R. and Quillfeldt, J., Chapter 8 (Standard of living) and Chapter 14 (The pound in your pocket) in *Economics Investigated*, Collins Educational, 1989.

Data Response

Inflation in the United Kingdom

This task is based on an examination question set by the Oxford & Cambridge Schools Examination Board in 1991. Study the two graphs, which are adapted from *Employment Gazette* and *UK Economics Analyst* respectively (both November 1990), and answer the questions.

Measuring inflation

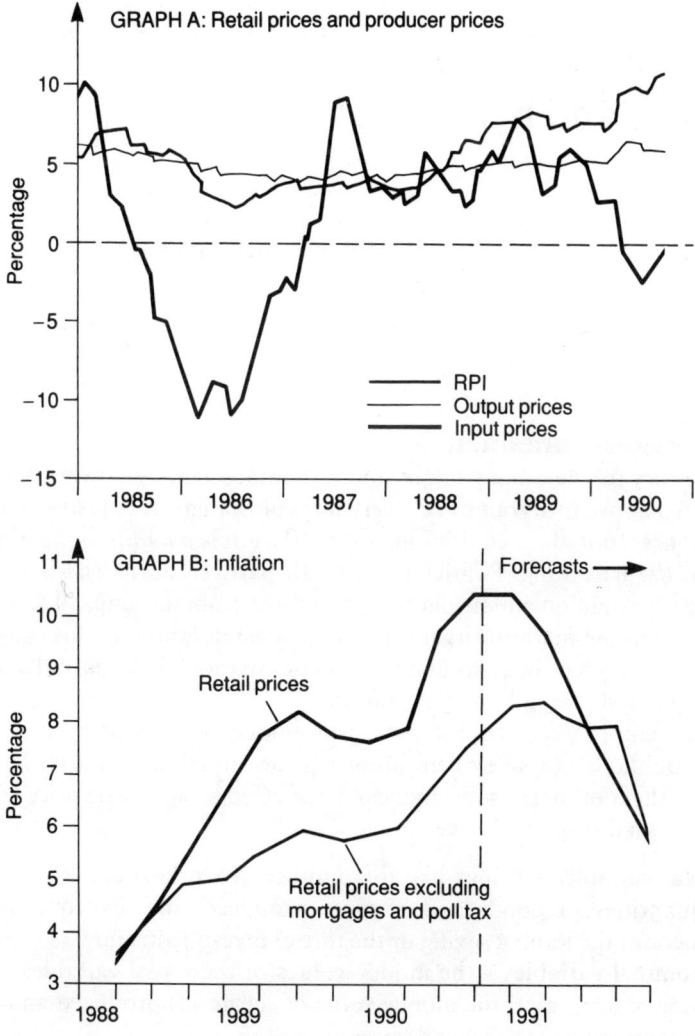

1. Define *input prices* and *output prices* and account for the divergence between the two series since 1985 (graph A).
2. How is the RPI calculated? Describe trends in the RPI since 1985 (graph A).
3. Does the calculation of inflation excluding mortgage interest and poll tax (community charge) give a more accurate and useful indication of the trend in inflation than changes in the RPI? (graph B). Explain your answer.
4. Account for the forecast trend in 1990/91 for the various measures of inflation in graph B.

Chapter Three
Costs and benefits of inflation

'Inflation is public enemy number one.'   Edward Heath, British Prime Minister, January 1973

Mistaken concensus?

Contrary to what many might think, the statement by Edward Heath quoted above turns out to be a very difficult statement to justify. He is, of course, not alone in thinking that inflation is *a bad thing*, perhaps even *the* bad thing. Politicians from all parties, journalists from all shades of opinion and media type, and those from the City, all seem to agree that the first priority is the fight against inflation. In this chapter we look at what the costs and benefits of inflation might be and assess their relative strengths and weaknesses.

As might be expected, the consensus among politicians and the general public is not so evident among professional economists. Many argue that nothing of substance can be affected by aggregate price level. There is a dichotomy between:

- **real variables** – things like the number of workers employed, the quantities of goods and services produced, the distribution of income, the level of saving or the rate of investment; and
- **nominal variables** – the money values of these real variables (e.g. money wage rate, the money value of the goods produced and the money value of saving and investment).

Confusion in the price mechanism

One argument is that, whilst one price level is much the same as any other, it is in *changing* from one level to another that the damage is done. Simply comparing two *steady states* – one with a low price level and one with a high price level – overlooks what happens in the transition from one state to the other. It is, of course, in this transitional period (whilst price level is changing) that inflation is occurring. *The economic damage sustained during this transition arises from our inability to distinguish between changes in aggregate price level and changes in relative prices*. Thus if producers see that customers are prepared to pay more for their products (i.e. product prices are rising), should they interpret this as an increase in the demand for their products and increase their production, as the price mechanism would suggest, or should they assume that all prices and wages are changing by the same amount and thus their product is no more in demand than before?

What is being suggested is that inflation causes confusion by making it difficult for economic agents correctly to perceive changes in relative prices. Correctly perceiving changes in relative prices is essential to the efficient operation of the price mechanism. When economic agents make mistakes we are all made worse off.

Uncertainty

This leads us on to the second argument for keeping inflation low – **uncertainty**. The reasoning is that inflation gives rise to uncertainty about the future, so investors are frightened off and productive capacity shrinks. This argument is very similar to the first one, but rests on whether agents actually believe forecasts of inflation. If they have doubts then they may become more cautious and not invest. This means that we must either keep inflation low enough not to be an important consideration, or we must be extremely convincing in our forecasts of inflation.

These are rather esoteric reasons for wanting to reduce inflation. In the popular mind the main problem is the damage done to those on 'fixed' incomes and those with savings.

Income and wealth distributions

Some people feel that they have carefully planned their lives, saved, invested in pension schemes and generally acted responsibly only to find that the value of their hard-earned savings and pensions has been eroded by unforeseen increases in the price level. If price level doubles their pensions and savings lose half their value.

With regard to pensioners, it is quite difficult to find anyone on a truly fixed income. Most pensions, including state pensions, are **index linked**. If the retail price index goes up by 10 per cent, then the pensions go up by that percentage. That is one reason why the government is so keen to get an accurate measure of retail price inflation.

Those who fear that their savings will be eroded can equally be reassured. When inflation occurs, the interest rates on savings deposits rise to cover the loss of value due to inflation and to pay the normal interest rate too. Of course it is not possible always to keep interest rates absolutely in line with inflation but, by and large, if the price mechanism is working properly, there should be no loss of value of savings from this source.

Menu and shoe-leather costs

Some economists speak of the **menu costs** and **shoe-leather costs** of inflation. By the former is meant that, as inflation gets higher and higher, sellers have to revise their price lists. No doubt it does cost something to keep on reprinting these price lists, but even so there can be no case here for saying that inflation is a major, or even an appreciable, cost to the economy.

Shoe-leather costs can be explained as follows. With high inflation, the amount of cash we hold for day-to-day transactions is losing value all the time. If we take £400 out of an interest-bearing account, intending to spend it through the coming month, then an inflation rate of 1 per cent a month would mean that the last £20 (spent in the last week) would be worth 20p less than when it was drawn out. This would encourage people to go to the bank more often so as to leave their money earning interest for as long as possible. The time and effort spent making these journeys to the bank are the 'shoe-leather' costs.

Exchange rates

A somewhat stronger argument for controlling inflation lies not within the economy but outside it. As the price level in the UK rises, UK goods become more and more expensive. In other countries, too, prices may be increasing, but if the UK inflation rate exceeds the rates elsewhere then UK goods will become progressively less and less competitive *vis à vis* those other countries. This loss of **competitiveness** leads to a loss of export sales and an increase in imports. The demand for UK goods declines both at home and abroad, so UK workers are laid off and factories close.

The increased imports and the decreased exports would create a trade deficit, and we can only run a trade deficit if we can pay for our excess imports out of our reserves of gold and foreign exchange. Obviously if we do not export enough to earn the necessary quantity of dollars to buy the US goods we are importing, then we have to make up the difference out of borrowings from abroad and from previously earned reserves. Eventually we would run out of reserves and fail to find any more foreigners who would be willing to lend to us, and so our trade deficit would become unsustainable.

When this happens it is necessary to reduce the value of our currency *vis à vis* other currencies.

Any inflation in the UK (which is not matched by inflation rates in our trading partners' countries) will put pressure on our exchange rate. If our exchange rate falls at the same rate as our price level rises, then our goods will keep constant export prices and leave foreign demand for our goods unchanged.

This realignment of currencies may be allowed to occur via the free operation of the foreign exchange markets or be managed by the government(s) concerned. The former is the case of free *floating* exchange rates, the latter is the case of the *fixed* exchange rate. Much economic policy choice depends upon which exchange rate regime – floating or fixed – is in operation. This will be taken further in Chapter 8. For the moment we note that inflation can only harm our foreign competitiveness if our exchange rate fails to follow the correct course.

Computational costs

First, although it is *possible* for agents to bear in mind the level of inflation when trying to discern changes in relative prices from changes in price level, it is quite difficult to do all the necessary computations all the time. We do our shopping with some idea in the back of our minds as to what constitutes a just price; for example, we do not expect to pay £2 for a pound of potatoes and would avoid shops which posted such prices. When there is inflation we have to constantly update all this information so that what was a fair price last year is not a fair price today. With an annual rate of inflation rate of, say 14.8 per cent, we have to be able to say what a just price for a pair of jeans would be today if it was £34.68 six months ago. These adjustments make perfect sense in theory but very little sense in practice.

Second, it could be argued that whereas it may be *possible* to protect interest rates, exchange rates and pensions etc. from the ravages of inflation, it all takes time and effort – sometimes a great deal of effort. Some could argue, therefore, that it might be simpler to control inflation.

Third, we have assumed above that the price mechanism is working well enough to maintain relative prices at their 'correct' levels, revise interest rates so that there is no tendency to penalize lenders over borrowers, and correct exchange rates so that there is no loss of international price competitiveness.

This is placing a huge burden on the price mechanism and many would argue that it is far too heavy. The price mechanism simply cannot keep up with anything more than very moderate rates of inflation. Some wage rates and salaries, for example, are very slow to change, and those who receive them suffer losses of real incomes during the

UK inflation

catch-up period. This loss of real incomes increases as the rate of inflation increases. Interest rates, too, are slow to change and have many influences on them apart from the need to correct the erosion of savings. This leads to savers objecting that their virtuous thrift is being penalised in favour of the profligate borrowers.

Similarly exchange rates, even when they are free to float, are influenced by capital flows and expected capital gains as well as price level, and simply do not change to maintain our international price competitiveness. UK exporters complain that inflation therefore leads to their losing sales and/or profits to low-inflation countries. Look at the UK's loss of competitiveness measured by the *real unit labour cost* in Figure 5.

Fourth, our system of income tax is not designed for an inflationary economy. Typically the amount of income tax we pay depends on our *nominal* (money) incomes, and the amount of capital gains tax depends on the increase in the *nominal* value of our assets. This means, for example, that we pay no income tax if our annual income is below, say, £4000; we then pay tax at a rate of 25 per cent for the next £20 000 and then at 40 per cent for the rest. Income tax paid by someone earning £60 000 per annum would be £19 400, which is 32.3 per cent of their income.

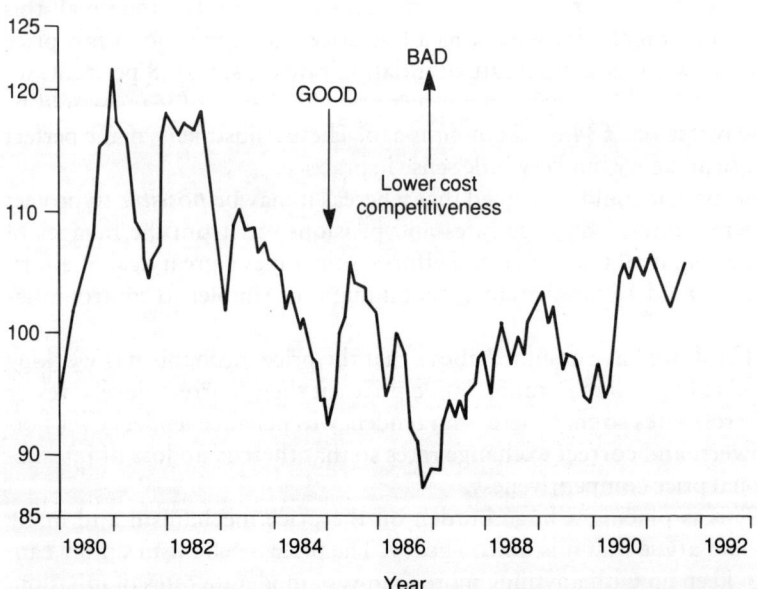

Figure 5 The UK's cost competitiveness – the real effective exchange rate based on relative normalized unit labour costs

Now assume that inflation occurs and price level doubles. Incomes double too, so that the £60 000 becomes £120 000 – remember all prices have been doubled so the real value of this pre-tax income has not changed. The income tax paid now, however, will be £43 400 (check the calculation), which is 36.2 per cent of income. Thus the tax to pay increases simply as a result of inflation, with no change in the structure of tax rates nor our *real* pre-tax income.

The effect is more dramatic for low-income families. If the income before inflation were just £4000, then no income tax would be paid; but after inflation this £4000 would double to £8000 and there would be a liability for £1000 in income tax, and so the real post-tax income would have fallen by 25 per cent.

Of course, the Chancellor of the Exchequer receives greater and greater tax revenues as inflation proceeds (this is called **fiscal drag**), but not everyone would like to see greater public revenues at the expense of the poorer members of our economy.

Similar arguments can be advanced about capital gains taxes. Were we to buy a painting for, say, £50 000 and its real value increased to £100 000, when we sold it we would have to pay capital gains tax on that increase in value. But if the real value remained unchanged whilst inflation increased its nominal value to £100 000, our real wealth would be unchanged but we would still have to pay capital gains tax on the increase in its *nominal* value. This was certainly not the intention of the tax nor does it seem particularly just.

By judiciously fiddling with the tax rates the government could no doubt do away with some of these unintended and unjust tax increases, but the fact remains that such changes are difficult and liable to error. The simplest solution may well be to keep inflation down to moderate levels.

Inflation: A good thing?

Some economists claim that mild inflation is positively beneficial to the economy. They argue that when we have some inflation it is easier for relative prices to adjust smoothly in response to market forces. This is because some prices and wages are very difficult to reduce in money terms. Unions resist cuts in money wages but seem to be less worried about cuts in *real* wages which come about when money wages rise slower than price level. Thus when there is inflation real wages can be reduced without the need to decrease money wage rates.

To see how this works, consider a market which is signalling a surplus of lawyers and a shortage of accountants. According to our theory the salaries of lawyers should fall relative to those of accountants. It turns out to be quite difficult to persuade lawyers (and others in surplus professions) to take cuts in salaries. There are wage contracts and agreements which cannot easily be broken. But, if we had a mild inflation (say 3 per cent a year) we could gradually reduce the real salaries of lawyers by simply not compensating them for the inflation. Thus mild inflation actually eases the the price mechanism.

That is all very well, say other economists, but mild inflation is likely to turn into hyperinflation and destroy the currency. Therefore, they say, have none of it. The facts, however, lend scant support to this claim. There have been inflations but very few have ever led to the destruction of a currency.

KEY WORDS

Real variables	Menu costs
Nominal variables	Shoe-leather costs
Price mechanism	Competitiveness
Relative prices	Exchange rates
Uncertainty	Computational costs
Index linked	Fiscal drag

Further reading

Eltis, W., 'How inflation undermines industrial success', *National Westminster Bank Review*, Feb. 1991.

'Inflation costs', *Lloyds Bank Economic Bulletin*, July 1991.

Maunder, P., Myers, D., Wall, N. and LeRoy Miller, Chapter 11 in *Economics Explained: A Coursebook in A-Level Economics*, 2nd edn, Collins Educational, 1991.

Paisley, R. and Quillfeldt, J., Chapter 3 (Yielding to the market) and Chapter 29 (Rags to riches) in *Economics Investigated*, Collins Educational, 1989.

Essay topics

1. What are the costs and benefits of inflation? Do the benefits of inflation ever justify a government allowing inflation to continue in an economy? (Associated Examining Board, 1990)
2. Distinguish between the domestic and external consequences of inflation. Which do you believe to be the more important in the UK? (University of Cambridge Local Examinations Syndicate, 1990)

3. 'There is no case for reducing the rate of inflation in the UK below the average rate prevailing in other advanced countries'. Do you agree? (University of Oxford Delegacy of Local Examinations, 1990)
4. Who, if anyone, gains from inflation? (Oxford & Cambridge Schools Examination Board, 1991)

Data Response

Household expenditure

This task is based on an examination question set by the University of London School Examinations Board in 1991. Examine Table A overleaf, which is taken from *Social Trends*, no. 2, published by HMSO in 1990.

1. Explain what is meant by the phrase 'indices at constant 1985 prices'.
2. With reference to the table, which category of consumer expenditure shows (a) the fastest and (b) the slowest rate of growth in the period shown?
3. Outline the reasons, other than changes in real income, for these contrasting growth rates.
4. What does the table suggest about the income elasticity of demand for (a) food, (b) the purchase of vehicles, and (c) TV and video?
5. What is the significance of the changing expenditure pattern for calculating the index of retail prices?
6. What are the implications of the data for the changing pattern of employment in the UK?

UK inflation

Table A

	1976	1981	1985	1986	1987	1988	£million in 1988 (current prices)
Indices at constant 1985 prices							
Food	96	98	100	103	103	103	36 687
Alcoholic drink	93	95	100	100	102	105	18 508
Tobacco	126	117	100	97	97	97	7 945
Clothing and footwear	67	78	100	108	116	122	19 791
Housing	84	92	100	103	107	111	42 993
Fuel and power	92	96	100	103	102	104	11 562
Household goods and services							
Household durables	81	85	100	106	109	120	9 711
Other	87	88	100	104	113	121	9 452
Transport and communication							
Purchase of vehicles	64	78	100	108	116	134	17 437
Running of vehicles	81	90	100	106	111	117	17 325
Other travel	82	92	100	106	118	127	9 986
Post and telecommunications	62	85	100	108	117	129	5 650
Recreation, entertainment and education							
TV, video, etc	55	72	100	114	123	133	6 413
Books, newspapers, etc	109	110	100	102	103	102	3 737
Other	82	94	100	105	113	120	15 946
Other goods and services							
Catering (meals, etc)	90	89	100	108	118	140	23 557
Other goods	89	86	100	107	116	127	12 292
Other services	57	73	100	112	126	133	14 999
Less expenditure by foreign tourists etc. in the UK	87	82	100	96	101	95	7 065
Household expenditure abroad	47	94	100	112	128	146	7 542
Total household expenditure	82	90	100	105	111	118	284 468

Costs and benefits of inflation

Percentage of total household expenditure at current prices							
Food	18.7	16.1	14.3	14.0	13.5	12.9	36 687
Alcoholic drink	7.7	7.4	7.5	7.1	6.8	6.5	18 508
Tobacco	4.2	3.7	3.3	3.2	3.0	2.8	7 945
Clothing and footwear	7.8	6.8	7.1	7.1	7.2	7.0	19 791
Housing	13.7	15.0	15.3	15.4	15.2	15.1	42 993
Fuel and power	4.8	5.1	5.1	4.8	4.4	4.1	11 562
Household goods and services	7.7	7.0	6.8	6.7	6.7	6.7	19 163
Transport and communication	15.2	16.8	17.0	16.7	17.2	17.7	50 398
Recreation, entertainment and education	9.3	9.4	9.4	9.5	9.4	9.2	26 096
Other goods, services, and adjustments	11.0	12.6	14.2	15.4	16.6	18.0	51 325
Totals	100.0	100.0	100.0	100.0	100.0	100.00	284 468

Chapter Four
Monetarist explanations

'Inflation is always and everywhere a monetary phenomenon.'
Professor Milton Friedman

The connection between money supply and inflation has already been hinted at in an earlier chapter. Indeed, the very early usage of the word 'inflation' meant an unmerited increase in the money supply. In this chapter we examine the theoretical justification for (and some historical facts in support of) the view that there is a stable relationship between the general level of prices and the quantity of money in the economy.

The quantity of money
To investigate whether money can cause inflation, consider the simple economy in which there are but three goods – bread, wine and cloth. Every two days the economy produces 20 loaves of bread, 10 litres of wine and 20 metres of cloth. Let there also be 60 gold coins. Furthermore, let 1 loaf exchange for ½ litre of wine and/or 1 metre of cloth. This specifies all the relative prices since it implies, of course, that ½ litre of wine will exchange for 1 metre of cloth. At the end of two days the goods are brought to market, and the 20 loaves are exchanged for 20 gold coins, the 10 litres of wine exchanged for 20 gold coins and the 20 metres of cloth exchanged for 20 gold coins. Thus the price of bread is 1 coin per loaf, the price of wine is 2 coins per litre and the price of cloth is 1 coin per metre. These prices ensure that the relative values of the three goods are maintained and that all the coins are used in the exchange – i.e. all the money is used as a medium of exchange.

Having sold their goods each producer has an 'income' of 20 gold coins, which in total is just enough to buy all the goods brought to market in the first place – provided that the prices have remained unchanged.

Thus the baker can use some coins to buy wine and the rest to buy cloth to get the consumption desired. All the coins are spent and so are available for the next round of market exchanges in two days' time.

Imagine next that there are 120 gold coins but just the same quantities of goods with the same relative values. Now when the goods are brought to market bread will fetch 2 coins per loaf, wine 4 coins per litre and cloth 2 coins per metre. This ensures that all the coins are used up and the relative prices are maintained. Each producer now has 40 coins to spend but, since all prices have doubled, they can buy only the same bundle of goods as before.

It is now possible to speak of the general price level. In terms of coins the general price level has doubled. And this seems to be the result of doubling the number of coins (all of which get used as the medium of exchange) with a constant level of production.

The velocity of circulation

The next thing to consider is what would happen if we went back to using only 60 coins but this time, instead of visiting the market every two days with two days' production, we visited it every day with one days' production. In this case there would be 10 loaves, 5 litres of wine and 10 metres of cloth. Assuming the same relative values as before, when these goods were brought to market and exchanged for the 60 coins, each loaf would sell for 2 coins, each litre of wine for 4 coins and each metre of cloth for 2 coins. This would exhaust the medium of exchange (60 coins). Thus all prices have doubled again but this time it was caused by increasing the frequency of exchange – the number of times producers received the 60 coins rose from seven times every two weeks (once every two days) to fourteen times every two weeks (once a day). This frequency is called the **velocity of circulation** of money, and doubling the velocity has the same effect as doubling the quantity. Each coin is asked to 'work' twice as hard.

The quantity theory of money

The relationship between the stock of money, the velocity of circulation and the general price level has been much examined and is given expression in two principal ways. The oldest is the **quantity equation** and is expressed as:

$$M \times V = P \times Y$$

where M is the quantity of money in the system, V is the velocity of circulation, P is the general level of prices, and Y is the quantity of goods being exchanged (assumed to be the number produced).

As expressed, this is not so much an equation as a truism – an **identity**. The left-hand side of the equation is the number of coins multiplied by the number of times they change hands per year. In other words it is the total value of expenditure in the economy. If between us we have 100

£1 coins, and we hand them over to someone else (buy something) 50 times in a year, the total *expenditure* in the economy in that year must be £5000.

The right-hand side of the quantity equation is the average price of all goods sold times the number sold. This must be the value of the total *sales* in the economy. The quantity equation therefore merely states the obvious and trivial fact that total purchases must equal total sales – you simply cannot have a sale without a purchaser.

The Fisher equation

The quantity equation is made operational – made useful – by adding some constraints to it. According to **Fisher**, after whom the equation is now named, the level of output Y and the velocity of circulation V have tendencies to stability. Output tends to return to its full-employment level and velocity tends to return to its equilibrium value. These equilibrium levels are set quite independently of money supply and are themselves slow to change.

If this is true, then the quantity theory tells us that price level varies with money supply. If money supply doubles then price level doubles too – it can do no other. Even if we consider the case where output is changing, it is still the case that if the quantity of money M increases faster than the quantity of goods Y, and if the velocity V remains constant, then price level P must rise. Information available from the Bank of England shows that the velocity of circulation, whether defined in terms of narrow money (M0) or broad money (M4), does not remain steady. The former has been *steadily rising* since 1960 whereas the latter has shown an erratic *decline*.

The Cambridge equation

The second version of the quantity theory is the **Cambridge equation.** This is much the same as the Fisher equation except that it is expressed immediately as an equation rather than being expressed first as an identity and then made operational by being constrained in some way.

The Cambridge approach (due mainly to **Pigou**) is to say that every year we have to conduct YP pounds-worth of transactions if we are to buy our national output Y at the aggregate price level P. In order to engage in that value of transactions, we need a certain amount of medium of exchange (M), and as the value of transactions rises so too does the necessary quantity of medium of exchange. Thus the Cambridge approach is in terms of a demand-for-money equation – how much money we want to make our transactions.

The relationship between the value of transactions and the quantity

Monetarist explanations

of medium of exchange is expressed as an equation:

$$M = k(Y \times P)$$

where k is a constant and is obviously equivalent to the reciprocal of V in the Fisher equation.

Thus there are two ways of expressing the quantity theory of money, but both yield the result that money and price level are related.

This is the kernel of the monetarist case. Monetarists argue that since output Y and velocity V (or k) change only slowly – if at all – then any change in price level P must be associated with a change in the quantity of money M. In other words, inflation is always and everywhere a *monetary phenomenon*. It is the government's job to ensure that the growth of money supply never exceeds the growth of output. If they go up at the same annual percentage rates, then price level will remain constant.

We shall look at the implications of this for monetary policy in Chapter 8. For the moment we simply note that monetarists link inflation with the quantity of money, and hence argue that the control of inflation means the control of money supply.

Some facts

So much for the theory. Is there any empirical evidence to support the fundamental monetarist claim?

In the mid-sixteenth century when coins – particularly of gold and silver – constituted the quantity of money in the economy, a French social philosopher (Jean Bodin) noticed that the rise in prices in France coincided with the influx of gold and silver from Spain, which in turn received them from the New World. Of course, many other things were happening at the same time and not all commentators agree that the inflation had its roots in the influx of precious metals; but the fact of its having happened remains.

Second, during the French Revolution citizens were issued with *assignats* – tokens to be used as money. These tokens were backed by land and were not related to the quantity of precious metals in France at the time. This issue of new currency greatly expanded money supply and coincided with an increase in the general level of prices.

Third, during the American Civil War southern states began issuing their own currencies in the form of banknotes. These Confederate banknotes were not backed by their equivalent value of precious metals. These notes – known as *greenbacks* – were issued somewhat extravagantly and tended to lose their value quickly. That is to say, the general level of prices expressed in terms of greenbacks rose as more greenbacks were issued.

UK inflation

The gold standard

Throughout most of our history we have either used precious metals for money or we have replaced the actual metal with paper banknotes. These notes were backed by gold so that banks were unable to issue more notes than they could support with their stocks of gold. This effectively prevented any undue expansion of money supply – it also, of course, prevented money supply expanding even when it was justified by an increase in output. This became known as the **gold standard**.

For a number of reasons, the UK and many other countries came off the gold standard and began issuing banknotes over and above the amount of gold they held. In the case of the UK this happened in September 1931. Some countries (Australia, New Zealand and South America) had preceded us, while others (Greece, Portugal and Japan) quickly followed. France held on until 1936. Since coming off the gold standard, there was a strong tendency for governments to issue too many notes and, again coincidentally, there was a noticeable increase in inflation rates.

This may seem pretty convincing, but it is a rather casual, unscientific way of analysing factual evidence. Of course, economists have adopted much more rigorous methods, but still there is no absolutely clear-cut case for saying that the monetarists have got it entirely right. Figure 6

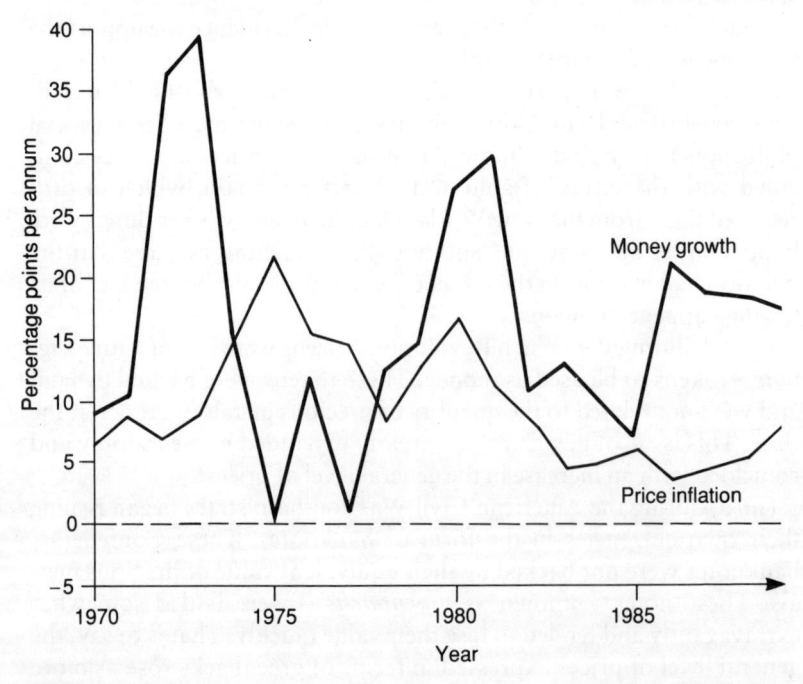

Figure 6 Money growth and price inflation in the UK, 1970–89

LETTERS TO *THE TIMES*
'Inadequacy' of the latest base rate cut

Sir: It seems the government is no longer pursuing a monetary policy with the object of achieving domestic stability. Previously, inflation was brought down from 21.9 per cent in May 1980 to 3.7 per cent in May 1983. This was done by using interest-rate policy to bring the rate of growth of broad measure of money supply (M3) under control. The exchange rate was allowed to float.

The growth of broad money (now called M4 on the new measure) rose from 13.5 per cent in 1986 to about 18 per cent in 1988, which level it remained until the spring of 1990. This was a signal that inflation would reappear, as it did.

Since October 1990 the growth of M4 has fallen rapidly to about 10 per cent per annum. With inflation still at over 6 per cent this means M4's real growth is only around 4 per cent; that is clearly inadequate.

This is the monetary signal which indicates that there is an urgent and overdue need for interest rate cuts. It merely confirms the evidence that we see and hear all around us that policy is far too tight. Today's half per cent cut is inadequate to put this right.

Our membership of the ERM is clearly resulting in the government using interest-rate policy to maintain a certain parity for the pound, and ignoring the needs of the domestic economy. Thus 527,000 jobs and many thousands of businesses have already been sacrificed on the alter of the ERM.

After three lost by-elections, and 900 lost council seats, I hope the government will now realise that the way to win the next election is to put the British economy first, to cut interest rates and leave the ERM.

Your faithfully,
NICHOLAS RIDLEY
MP for Cirencester and Tewkesbury (Con)
House of Commons
London SW1
24 May 1990

© Times Newspapers Ltd, 1990

Inflation and M3

Sir: Mr Nicholas Ridley (May 25) is attempting to perpetuate the dangerous myth that in the early eighties there was a monetarist miracle which was subsequently betrayed. His claim is that there was a big reduction of inflation between 1980 and 1983 and that this occurred because the money supply had been brought under control.

But money growth was not brought under control in the early eighties. The growth in M3 actually accelerated between 1978–9 and 1981–2, and although it fell back a little in 1982–3, it was still higher than it had been in 1978–9, immediately before Mrs Thatcher came to power. Moreover, money growth in the early Thatcher years was above the top of its target range in all years but one; it was enormously above the targeted range during Mr Ridley's halcyon period.

It is extremely misleading, to use no stronger word, of Mr Ridley arbitrarily to select, for his inflation comparisons, May 1980 (a peak) and May 1983 (a trough). The acceleration of inflation in the year ending May 1980 was largely the direct and indirect result of the rise in indirect tax rates which the government itself had imposed.

Whatever it was that produced the May 1983 trough, it wasn't the money supply. In any case, the 1983 deceleration was momentary; inflation was back to 7 per cent in 1985.

It is true that inflation fell right back in 1986, but this was surely the result of a 7 per cent fall in import prices combined with unemployment in excess of three million. It can hardly have had anything to do with M3 which, having grown at an average rate of 14 per cent since 1979, grew by 16.4 per cent in 1985–6.

Yours faithfully
WYNNE GODLEY
University of Cambridge
Department of Applied Economics
Sidgwick Avenue, Cambridge
26 May 1991

© Times Newspapers Ltd, 1991

shows how money supply and price inflation behaved in the UK between 1970 and 1989, and it is not clear from this that 'inflation is always and everywhere a monetary phenomenon'. There are, as we shall see, many different explanations which fit these same 'facts' equally well.

KEY WORDS

Velocity of circulationFisher
Quantity theory of moneyCambridge equation
Quantity equationPigou
IdentityGold standard

Further reading
Driffill, J., 'The current state of UK monetary policy', *Economic Review*, Jan. 1987.
Reddaway, B., 'Testing monetarist theory', *Economic Review*, Sept. 1989.
Trevithick, J.A., Chapter 5 in *Inflation*, Pelican, 1988.
Turner, P., 'Monetary growth and inflation', *Economic Review*, Jan. 1991.

Essay topics
1. Why might the government consider control of the money supply to be an essential component of economic policy? (University of London Schools Examination Board, 1987)
2. 'Inflation is caused solely because there is too much money in the economy'. Do you agree? (University of Cambridge Local Examinations Syndicate, 1989)
3. What causes inflation within an economy? What are the consequences of inflation for an economy? (University of Cambridge Local Examinations Syndicate, 1987)
4. Is monetarism based on the belief that the economy is inherently stable? (Oxford & Cambridge Schools Examination Board, 1988)

Data Response Question 3

Money and inflation

This task is based on an examination question set by the University of Oxford Delegacy of Local Examinations in 1989. Examine Table A (reproduced from *Economic Trends*, 1988) which shows the growth of the UK economy between 1978 and 1987. All the figures other than those for unemployment are year-on-year percentage changes. The unemployment figures are percentages of the total labour force who are unemployed.

TABLE A

	Retail prices	Money stock (£M3)	GDP at factor cost at 1980 prices	Unemployment rate	Average earnings (whole economy)	Output per person employed	Import prices (unit value)
	(per cent growth rate)			(%)	(per cent growth rate)		
1978	8.3	15.6	2.9	4.7	N/a	2.7	3.6
1979	13.4	13.2	2.7	4.3	15.3	1.9	6.9
1980	17.9	18.8	−2.3	5.4	11.9	−2.1	10.0
1981	11.9	25.2	−0.9	8.5	12.9	2.0	8.2
1982	8.6	9.0	1.6	9.9	9.4	3.6	7.9
1983	4.6	11.2	3.3	10.7	8.4	3.9	9.3
1984	5.0	10.0	2.4	11.1	6.1	1.5	9.6
1985	6.1	13.4	3.6	11.3	8.5	2.1	3.9
1986	3.4	18.8	3.1	11.5	7.9	2.5	−7.7
1987	4.2	21.8	4.3	10.4	7.8	3.4	2.8

1. To what extent do the data in the table support a monetary theory of inflation?
2. How would you account for the course of inflation in the United Kingdom over this period?

Chapter Five
The Keynesian view

'As soon as output has increased sufficiently to begin to reach 'bottlenecks' there is likely to be a sharp rise in the prices of certain commodities.' John Maynard Keynes, *The General Theory*

The Keynesian view is named after one of the most famous economists of the twentieth century. John Maynard Keynes (later Lord Keynes) followed his father (John Neville Keynes) into economics and, after publishing books on statistics and money, in 1936 published his revolutionary economic views in his *General Theory of Employment, Interest and Money.* In the *General Theory,* Keynes sought to show that many of the unemployed workers at the time were the result of the failure of the price mechanism properly to govern the economy. As part of this argument he advanced two propositions which together effectively destroyed the monetarist's theoretical link between money supply and price level.

Store of value
His first point is that money is used not only as a **medium of exchange** but also as a **store of value.** Many people save some of their income and their accrued wealth has to be held in some way. They could buy stocks and shares or government securities or land or even old masters, but with each of these there is some risk. Stocks and shares can lose value overnight, and the value of an old master depends on capricious fashion – and so the saver could find old age approaching with nothing much to live off. When there was reason to believe that the values of these assets were becoming questionable, savers looked for some absolutely safe way of holding their wealth. An obvious candidate was money. Money may not yield a return like interest, capital gains or dividends, but at least its value remains intact. So why take the chance? Why not hold some or all of the wealth as money?

This means that not all the money in the economy will be engaged as a medium of exchange. Some notes and coins will be taken to market and exchanged for goods each day, but some notes and coin will find their

The Keynesian view

Main money measures fail the test

Where have all the monetarists gone? One striking contrast between the current UK recession and the economic downturn of 1979-81 is the relatively low weight now attached to monetary indicators, as the Treasury and private commentators try to judge the course of the economy.

Things were different in the early Eighties, the height of the monetarist experiment. Then, every twitch in the money supply measures was scanned to assess whether inflation was beaten and growth would resume. The Chancellor has said he prefers survey evidence as a guide, although the latest CBI industrial trends data need careful interpretation to fit his optimistic view of the economic outlook.

In the past 10 years, there has been mounting scepticism over the usefulness of monetary measures as targets for policy and as indicators of economic activity. While the authorities retain an M0 target, this appears to be only for form's sake, since the Chancellor routinely relates his interest-rate decisions to two other factors: inflation and sterling's position in the ERM.

When money supply was targeted, the results were unsatisfactory. Financial deregulation distorted the target measures. Worse still, the broad correlation between the targets and the objective variables – such as inflation or nominal GDP – seemed to break down in a vicious demonstration of Goodhart's Law. Named after an eminent Bank of England economist, this states that any previously observed relationship between one variable and another disappears as soon as the authorities choose to target one of the variables with a view to achieving a desired outcome for the other.

It is therefore understandable that the Chancellor prefers to target inflation itself without looking too closely at intermediate monetary variables. The very fact that he has moved in this direction, however, may well mean that the reverse of Goodhart's Law now applies. With money supply no longer targeted, it might well give important signals on the state of the economy.

A glance at the data for M0 and M4, however, hardly gives support to this view. M0 growth has fluctuated unevenly over the past four years (see chart). M0 comprises notes and coin in circulation and banks' operational balances with the Bank of England, so it responds to those factors which affect demand for currency. These include not only the general demand for goods and services, mostly small-ticket items which are typically paid for in cash, but also pay trends in such industries as construction, where a lot of casual labour is paid in cash. The interplay of these factors is sometimes hard to interpret, particularly when such external shocks as a VAT rise can increase the demand for currency. The present sluggishness in M0 is particularly disturbing as an indicator of demand for casual labour and for small retail items, since it comes after the VAT increase in the Budget, which should have added around 1 per cent to M0.

M4, which includes notes and coin in circulation and all domestic sterling deposits with banks and building societies, has also had its shortcomings in recent years. It gave no inkling that a recession was on the way until the third quarter of 1990 – about the time the Government and financial markets woke up to the possibility. Prior to 1990, M4 had been growing consistently at a double-figure rate, without appearing to portend any serious risk of overheating in the economy. Strong M4 growth co-existed with 3 per cent inflation in 1987 and 10 per cent inflation in 1990.

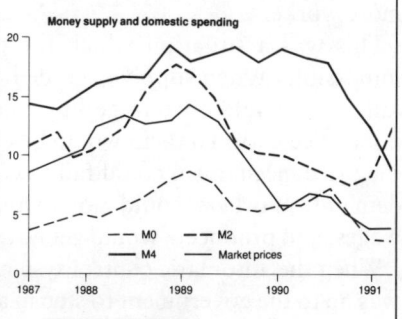

Money supply and domestic spending

STEPHEN LEWIS
Source: *Independent on Sunday*
4 August 1991

way into the portfolios of wealth holders. Money held in idle balances is not part of the circulating medium of exchange and so will not affect price level. In some cases and at some times, Keynes argued, the public's demand for money to hold as wealth will be very great indeed and the government can issue as much as it likes without there being any increase in medium of exchange or, consequently, of the price level.

Fluctuating output

The second point made by Keynes was the output was not constant as the monetarists argued. Output does change, and changes quite a lot even in the short run. He was writing at a time when output was very low and demonstably not constant. If the government followed the monetarist's prescription and kept money supply constant even when output was falling rapidly, then – even according to their own theory – the general level of prices would rise. In this case it was not the increase in money supply that caused the price level to rise, it was the fall in output. Thus it was no longer quite so straightforward to connect money supply M with price level P because other things were changing too.

This is the destructive element of what Keynes had to say – he was denying the monetarist case. What remains to be done is to formulate an alternative explanation of inflation.

Aggregate demand

To follow this part of the story it is necessary to understand something of the Keynesian explanation of unemployment. Keynes argued that employers were unable to hire the unemployed workers because they could find no buyers for their goods. There was a general lack of **aggregate demand.** There were too few buyers in the market so that goods were left unsold and producers cut back on production and laid off more workers.

This was a situation which the pre-Keynesians had dismissed as impossible. When supply exceeded demand, prices were supposed to fall. This would encourage buyers and discourage producers so the imbalance between them would be corrected. But Keynes showed that the price mechanism could fail to correct this deficiency in aggregate demand. Workers could not increase demand by accepting lower wages, and producers would get nowhere by simply cutting prices.

When the automatic control system – the price mechanism – failed it was up to the government to step in and do something.

The Keynesian solution was for the government to make up for the deficiency of aggregate demand by increasing its own expenditure. He urged governments to spend more when times were hard. They should

The Keynesian view

LETTERS TO *THE INDEPENDENT*
Monetarist doubts about a UK economic recovery

Sir: Christopher Huhne's article ("Despondency is a minority taste", 15 October) regarding the accuracy of monetarists' predictions conceals more than it reveals. Those whom he attacks have scored consistently well in his famous annual forecasting competition, not least Professor Tim Congdon.

Mr Huhne's thesis appears to be that if an economic relationship is any less reliable than an engineering constant, then it should be discarded. Monetary signals have been very difficult to interpret in the 1980s for all the reasons stated in his article; the argument is between those who are keen to learn from the past and those who are not. In the UK, students of narrow (M0) and broad money (M4) can agree that a formidable deflation of the economy is in progress and that, in some respects, credit and money developments are similar to those that preceded the depression of 60 years ago.

The fundamental issue, which divides economists of all persuations, is whether inflation or economic growth will be the lasting casualty of this monetary deflation. In fiercely competitive manufacturing industries, there should be little doubt that prices will bear the brunt; but in consumer services and distributive industries, the greater threat is to output and employment.

If the unwinding of the credit cycle brings a parallel destruction of economic capacity, then stagnation and inflation can co-exist. Lord Rees-Mogg is amply justified in alerting the readers of *The Independent* to the danger that this "economic recovery" will prove to be yet another false dawn.

Yours faithfully,
PETER WARBURTON
Dunstable, Bedfordshire
15 October 1991

Sir: William Rees-Mogg concluded an article, published by *The Independent* on 7 October, with the words:

the monetarists were right about the Barber inflation, the success of the early Thatcher disinflation, the Lawson inflation and the current recession. We could be right again.

I am determined that the record should be kept straight, as important questions of economic theory, forecasting methodology and the conduct of economic policy are at issue. William Rees-Mogg is not entitled to claim that he was among those who were "right" about the Barber débâcle because, in the editorial columns of *The Times*, he was an active, indeed rhetorical, supporter of the government at that time. So far as I know, my own (Keynesian) Economic Policy Group were the only academics who publicly opposed the Barber boom root and branch.

Lord Rees-Mogg's second claim is framed ambiguously; did he mean that the early Thatcherite disinflation was a success or that it had successful features? Presumably he is referring to the fact that inflation fell from 10.5 per cent in early 1979 to 4 per cent in the middle of 1983. But this cannot have anything to do with earlier changes in the money supply, which had not been at all successfully controlled and had been enormously higher than 4 per cent.

I have already pointed out, in a letter published by The *Independent* on 27 October 1989, that Lord Rees-Mogg was using incorrect figures in support of this particular claim. Meanwhile, I stick to my opinion that the fall in inflation in 1983 was the result of the fall in the price of oil, and more important, the rise in unemployment from 1.1 million to 2.75 million. I take it that this rise in unemployment does not score as an early Thatcherite success?

I am not clear how many people criticised the Lawson boom at the time it was occurring; did Lord Rees-Mogg do so? It was very widely hailed as a miracle at the time, and had much to do with the Conservative victory at the last general election. Whoever did criticise the Lawson boom, the monetarists certainly had no monopoly. For instance, it was I who first, in February 1988, used the expression "Miracle or Mirage", which was subsequently pinched by the BBC.

Again, monetarists have no monopoly in having predicted the present collapse. My (Keynesian) Cambridge colleagues and I have been predicting it for the past two years at least.

As it happens, I agree with Lord Rees-Mogg that no recovery – certainly not a recovery large enough to bring down unemployment – is in prospect. But what would he now do about it? Increase the money supply? Drop out of the EMS?

Yours faithfully,
WYNNE GODLEY
Jerome Levy Economics Institute
Bard College
Annadale-on-Hudson
New York
15 October 1991

43

not tighten their belts but should spend their way out of recessions. At the time this proved a very popular policy and was adopted more or less throughout the free world.

According to Keynesian theories, this increased government expenditure could be financed though the issuing of new money. The UK was no longer on the *gold standard* and had full control over its money stock. Expansion was an easy, painless and effective way back to full employment.

This was radical enough to constitute a revolution in economic thought and economic policy. The whole focus of the government's policy was changed from one of controlling money supply (monetary policy) to one of controlling aggregate demand through its own expenditure (fiscal policy).

Inflationary and deflationary gaps

The problem, of course, was to know when and by how much to expand. If they expanded too little then supply would still outrun demand and workers would be unnecessarily unemployed (the **deflationary gap**). If they expanded too much then demand would exceed supply and this excess demand would lead to a price rise (the **inflationary gap**).

These 'gaps' are illustrated in Figure 7. Aggregate demand (Y_d) in a

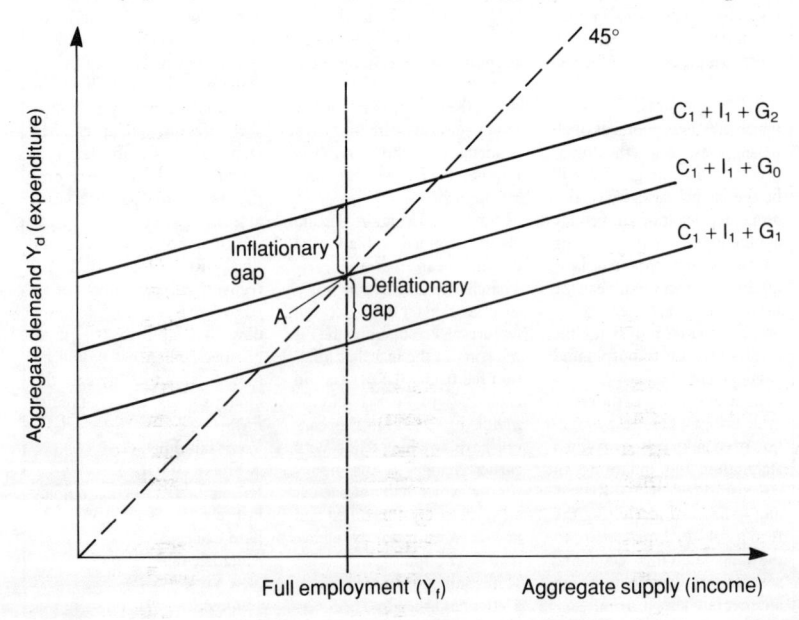

Figure 7 The inflationary and deflationary gaps

closed economy is made up of consumers' expenditure C which increases with income, investment I which remains constant, and government expenditure G:

$$Y_d = C + I + G$$

Since C increases with income Y, so will aggregate demand increase with income – so the graph of Y_d against Y slopes upwards. The 45° line represents all points where aggregate demand Yd equals income Y. Income is generated by, and hence is equal to, the supply of goods and services, and hence when aggregate demand equals income it also equals aggregate supply. The intersection of the aggregate demand line Y_d with the 45° line (point A) is where the economy settles down. To the left of point A, aggregate demand is greater than supply so output will be increased to meet that excess demand. To the right of A, supply exceeds demand so output will be cut. At point A there is no tendency to increase or decrease output – it is an equilibrium.

The government can change its expenditure G, and thus move the aggregate demand curve up and down. This causes the equilibrium point to move to the right when G is increased and to the left when G is reduced. The government can therefore choose a level of output by choosing expenditure G. Obviously output is limited by scarce resources, so not all levels of output can be reached. The aim is to reach the level of output associated with a fully employed economy – this is shown as point Y_f in the figure. If the economy settles down at a point below Y_f there will be unemployed resources – the deflationary gap. When the point of intersection is above Y_f there is too much demand and we have an inflationary gap.

In times of unemployment, when demand is lower than supply, sellers of labour will be competing for jobs and sellers of goods will be competing for customers, and so there will be no tendency to increase either wages or prices. As demand is expanded, producers respond by hiring more workers and increasing output. Quantities, rather than wages and prices, respond. As demand is increased still further the full-employment (capacity) level of output is approached. At this point employers begin competing for the few remaining unemployed workers, and so wage rates will be bid up and up. Since some producers will reach their capacity, they will be unable to respond to further increases in demand by raising their output, and instead respond by raising prices.

This increase in the prices of individual goods clearly becomes general as demand is increased still further and more and more producers reach capacity. This economy-wide increase in prices results in increases in the general level of prices – i.e. inflation.

UK inflation

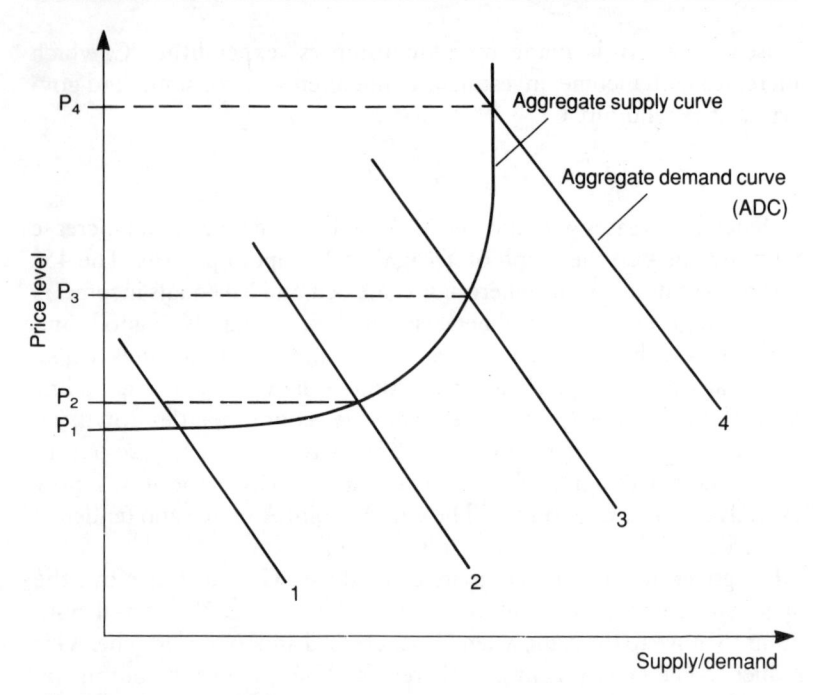

Figure 8 Aggregate supply and demand curves

Another way of illustrating this it to show how aggregate demand and aggregate supply change with aggregate price level (Figure 8). As to the aggregate supply curve, it will be upward sloping. At first, as supply increases, there will be only small increases in price, but after full-employment output is reached any further increase in supply will cause price to rise steeply.

On the demand side, the curve will be downward sloping – aggregate demand will fall as price rises. Thus we have two curves – one upward sloping and one downward sloping – and their intersection determines equilibrium levels of output and price.

The aggregate demand curve can be moved around by the government changing its expenditure. When output and employment are low (aggregate demand curve 1) the government can move the demand curve rightwards (ADC_2) to increase output with little or no effect on price level (P_1 to P_2). If, however, the demand curve is moved further to the right, the effect will be to increase price level (P_2 to P_3). Any further attempt to increase demand will lead to large price rises (P_3 to P_4) with little or no increase in output.

Thus, according to Keynes, inflation occurs when the government expands aggregate demand beyond our capacity to produce. It is excess

The Keynesian view

demand via **fiscal policy** rather than excess money through monetary policy which is at the heart of the inflation problem. To quote Keynes:

> 'It is probable that the general level of prices will not rise very much as output increases, so long as there are available efficient unemployed resources of every type. But as soon as output has increased sufficiently to begin to reach 'bottlenecks', there is likely to be a sharp rise in the prices of certain commodities.'

The Phillips curve

The above was about as formal a statement as Keynes made on the subject, and it was left to A.W. Phillips to take the matter further. Phillips examined the relationship between the rate of change of money wage rates (**wage inflation**) and the level of unemployment in the UK spanning the years 1861–1957. This relationship is shown in Figure 9.

The rate of wage inflation is the proportion of the total labour force which is unemployed in that year. (If there are 24 million workers available in the economy but only 20 million jobs, then there will be four million unemployed, which equals 16.6 per cent).

Phillips found that when unemployment was high, wage inflation was

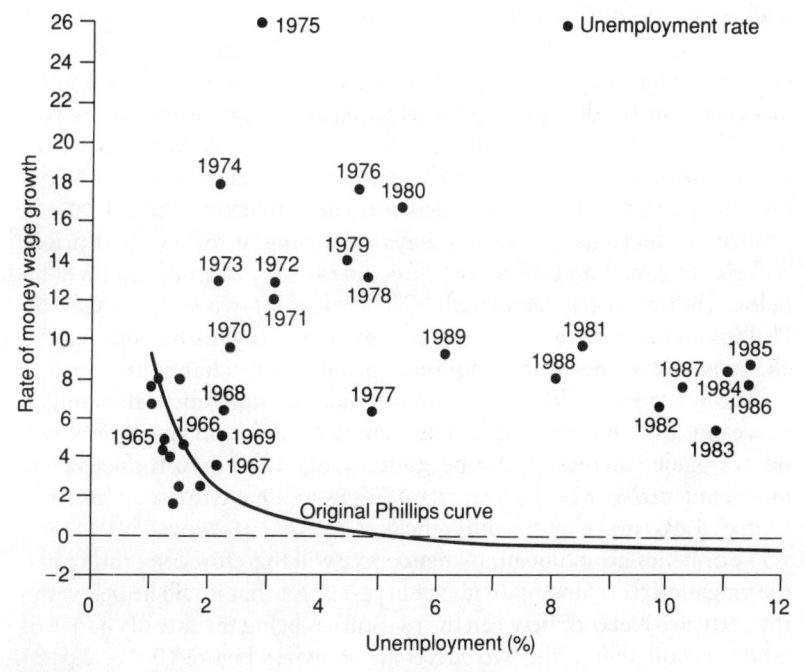

Figure 9 Unemployment and wage inflation in the UK

47

low. As the economy expanded and unemployment fell, then wage inflation rose – slowly at first but faster and faster as unemployment fell further and further. This (non-linear) relationship backs up the words of Keynes in that the level of unemployment is a measure of how close the economy is to full-employment (capacity) output, and as this is approached so prices will begin to rise.

This curve, of course, is in terms of wage rates and unemployment, whereas we are interested in the causes of **price inflation**, not *wage* inflation. The next step is therefore to forge a link between the money wage rate and the aggregate price index.

Labour productivity

Wages are clearly part of a producer's costs, and as costs rise then, to cover that increase, revenue must increase too. The revenue received by a producer depends on the price of the product and the quantity sold. In order to increase revenue, it is necessary either to produce more output *with the same labour force* or increase the price of the product.

The output per employee is called the **labour productivity** and there is a steady increase in labour productivity over time. Thus if labour productivity increases at the same rate as wages, then all the additional labour costs could be met out of increased sales. There would be no need for any price increase. But if the rate of change of wages exceeded that of labour productivity, then the difference would have to be made up by increasing the product price. This is the reason for saying we cannot pay ourselves more than we produce and for asking wage settlements to stay within the productivity limits. Provided we keep wage rises at or below the rate of productivity change there is no need to increase prices.

Since productivity is almost always increasing, it follows that prices will rise by less than wages, and thus the rate of *price* inflation will lie below the rate of *wage* inflation. Therefore, if we wish to use the Phillips curve to see what happens to price inflation as unemployment changes, all we need do is subtract productivity change from wage inflation. For example, if there is 2 per cent unemployment the Phillips curve tells us that there will be 3 per cent wage inflation (wage rates will on average be increasing at 3 per cent a year). If labour productivity is increasing at 2 per cent a year, then prices will have to go up by 1 per cent a year to make up the difference.

The price-inflation/unemployment curve will therefore look rather like the wage-inflation/unemployment curve, except that it will lie below it – the vertical difference between the two curves being the rate of change of labour productivity. The two curves are shown in Figure 10.

The net result of all this is that, according to Keynesians, the general

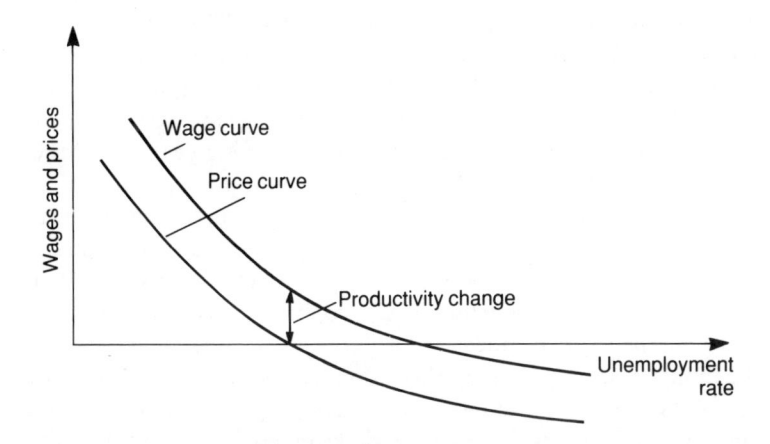

Figure 10 Productivity change

level of prices is not determined by the amount of money in the economy but by the amount of aggregate demand.

Breakdown of the Phillips curve

Faith in the Phillips curve, and in the Keynesian analysis of inflation, took a severe knock in the 1970s when very high inflation rates were experienced at the same time as there was very high unemployment (see Figure 9). Between 1967 and 1975 there was an enormous rise in wage inflation (from 4 to 26 per cent) with little or no change in unemployment. Since 1975, wage inflation has been falling but unemployment rates grew and grew. This conjunction of high inflation and high unemployment is called **stagflation**.

Stagflation is problematic for Keynesians since, if there is high unemployment there must be deficient aggregate demand; if there is deficient aggregate demand there can be no upward pressure on prices and wages; therefore there can be no inflation: *but there was*.

The decline of the popularity of the Phillip's curve was accelerated by the re-emergence of the monetarist view. Monetarists now argued that the level of employment, and hence the level of unemployment, is determined by the level of *real* wages. This means there can be no trade-off between unemployment and *money* wages. Their theory certainly leads them to this conclusion and, after 1974, there is some empirical support for them; but there remains the evidence of the original Phillip's curve.

To explain this away, monetarists suggest that workers will offer to work more if they *think* their real wages have been increased. This would be the case, for example, if they thought that price level would

UK inflation

increase by less than their money wage increased. The argument goes like this. Workers (or their trades unions) are offered a 10 per cent increase in money wage and invited to sign annual employment contracts on the basis of that money wage. At this stage the workers do not know what will happen to price level in the coming year, but if they expect it to remain constant then they will see the 10 per cent increase in money wages as a 10 per cent increase in real wages. They will offer more worker-hours and employment will increase. They will soon find out that they were wrong about price level – it actually rose by 10 per cent too – so real wages remain unchanged, but by then it is too late for them to rewrite their contracts.

The monetarists are arguing, therefore, that the Phillip's curve is the result of workers forming wrong expectations about price increases. Employment, they argue, really is determined by real wage – but *expected* real wage rather than actual real wage.

They go on to say that eventually workers will learn from their mistakes and begin to expect price increases, and when they do the Phillips curve breaks down – just as it did in the 1970s.

Expectations-augmented Phillips curve

The story gets worse. Once workers expect 10 per cent inflation they will want a 10 per cent increase in money wages just to maintain their expected real wages. In their wage negotiations they will need 10 per cent more just to keep worker-hours (employment) at last year's level. To get them to increase worker-hours (employment) they would have to be offered a 20 per cent increase in money wages. They would then discover that inflation rose to 20 per cent rather than the expected 10 per cent and their real wage would be what it was before.

The point is that the Phillips curve depends on what workers expect future inflation rates to be. If they expect no inflation then the relationship between employment and inflation will look like the original Phillips curve, but if workers expect 10 per cent inflation then the whole curve moves up by 10 per cent. If they expect 20 per cent then the curve moves up by 20 per cent. These 'stacked' Phillips curves are called **expectations-augmented Phillips curves** (see Figure 11) and are due to work of monetarists such as Friedman among others.

The natural rate of unemployment

As we have seen, employment is increased when workers underestimate inflation and is decreased when they overestimate inflation – that is what gives the Phillips curves their lengths. If workers correctly estimated inflation – i.e. their expectations turned out to be correct – they

The Keynesian view

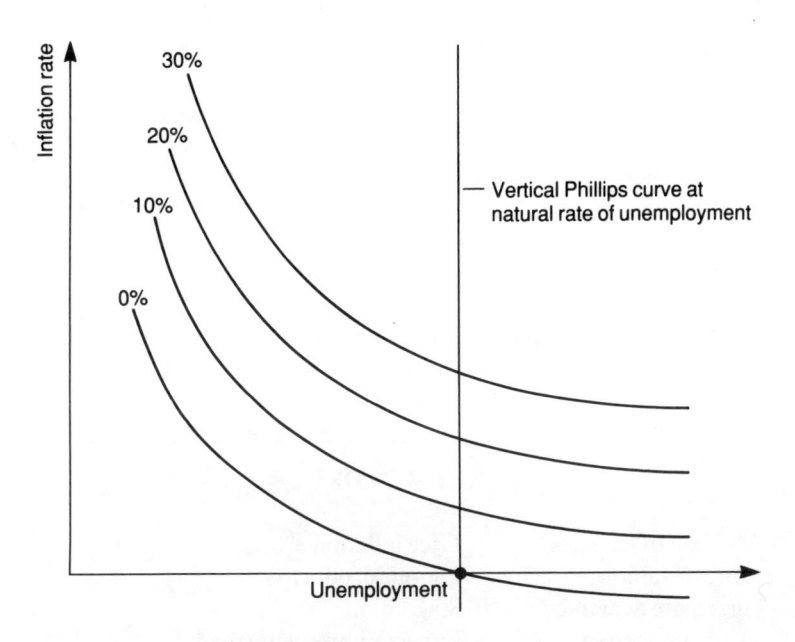

Figure 11 Expectations-augmented Phillips curves

would offer the *right* amount of labour and this *right* amount is called the **natural rate of employment** and the unemployment associated with it is called the **natural rate of unemployment**. Since this level of unemployment is the only rate compatible with correct expectations, all other combinations of unemployment and inflation rate must occur when expectations are wrong. The Phillips 'curve' when expectations are correct is therefore a vertical straight line – often referred to as the **vertical Phillips curve.**

The vertical Phillips curve obviously occurs at the natural rate of unemployment, and the natural rate can be found by examining the data on unemployment and price inflation in the original Phillips curve. That curve was constructed when workers expected an inflation rate of zero. The natural rate of unemployment would therefore be that level of unemployment at which these expectations proved correct; that is to say, at that level of unemployment at which inflation would actually be zero. When actual price inflation is zero their expectations would be correct. This, according to the work of Paish, occurs when unemployment is between 2 and 2.5 per cent, so the natural rate of unemployment is about 2.25 per cent – or at least that was the natural rate between 1948 and 1964.

Were we to construct a curve relating unemployment to price inflation for a period when workers expected 10 per cent price inflation, then the natural rate would occur at that level of unemployment at which inflation was 10 per cent. Since this expectations-augmented curve lies everywhere 10 per cent above the original curve, it too will yield a natural rate of unemployment of 2.25 per cent. At 2.25 per cent, this curve will predict a 10 per cent inflation rate, which is exactly what was expected.

The natural rate of unemployment therefore remains constant even though the curve is moving higher and higher as expected inflation gets higher and higher. This is shown in Figure 11.

There remains the question of just how workers form expectations about inflation. This turns out to be very important and will be taken up in Chapter 7.

KEY WORDS

Medium of exchange	Price inflation
Store of value	Labour productivity
Aggregate demand	Stagflation
Deflationary gap	Expectations-augmented
Inflationary gap	Phillips curve
Fiscal policy	Natural rate of
Wage inflation	(un)employment
Phillips curve	Vertical Phillips curve

Further reading

Clark, A. and Layard, R., *UK Unemployment*, Heinemann Educational, 1990.

Driffill, J., 'Inflation and the labour market', *Economic Review*, Jan. 1990.

Paisley, R. and Quillfeldt, J., Chapter 12 (Keynesians and monetarists) in *Economics Investigated*, Collins Educational, 1989.

Sumner, M., 'The Phillips curve', *Economic Review*, May 1984.

Trevithick, J.A., Chapter 4 in *Inflation*, Pelican, 1988.

Turner, P., 'Wages, prices and inflation', *Economic Review*, May 1988.

Essay topics

1. Discuss whether it is possible to have a low rate of unemployment at the same time as a low rate of inflation. (Associated Examining Board, 1990)
2. Explain carefully what you understand by inflationary and deflationary gaps. Describe, explain and evaluate policies which the

government may use to reduce the rate of inflation in the economy. (University of Cambridge Local Examinations Syndicate, 1989)
3. 'Any trade-off between the level of unemployment and the rate of inflation is a short-run phenomenon; in the long run there is no trade off.' Consider this view. (Welsh Joint Education Committee, 1990)
4. Does the experience of the 1980s show that the level of unemployment has no impact on the rate of inflation? (University of Oxford Delegacy of Local Examinations, 1987)
5. 'The Phillips curve is no longer relevant to economic policy.' Discuss. (University of London School Examinations Board, 1988)
6. Discuss the differences between 'monetarist' and 'Keynesian' views with regard to the significance of the quantity of money on macro-economic behaviour of economies. (Welsh Joint Education Committee, 1991)

Data Response

Production costs and prices

This task is based on an examination question set by the Oxford & Cambridge Schools Examination Board in 1990. Graphs A–C are taken from *Employment Gazette* for September 1989. They show percentage changes over the previous years. Study the graphs and answer the questions.

1. Describe the trend in average earnings since 1980.
2. Account for the growing divergence between the output series and the output-per-person-employed series after 1984.
3. Account for the volatility of input prices.
4. Why are the fluctuations in input prices not wholly reflected in output prices?
5. Use the data to account for movements in the RPI series since 1985. What other factors might have influenced the RPI over this period?

UK inflation

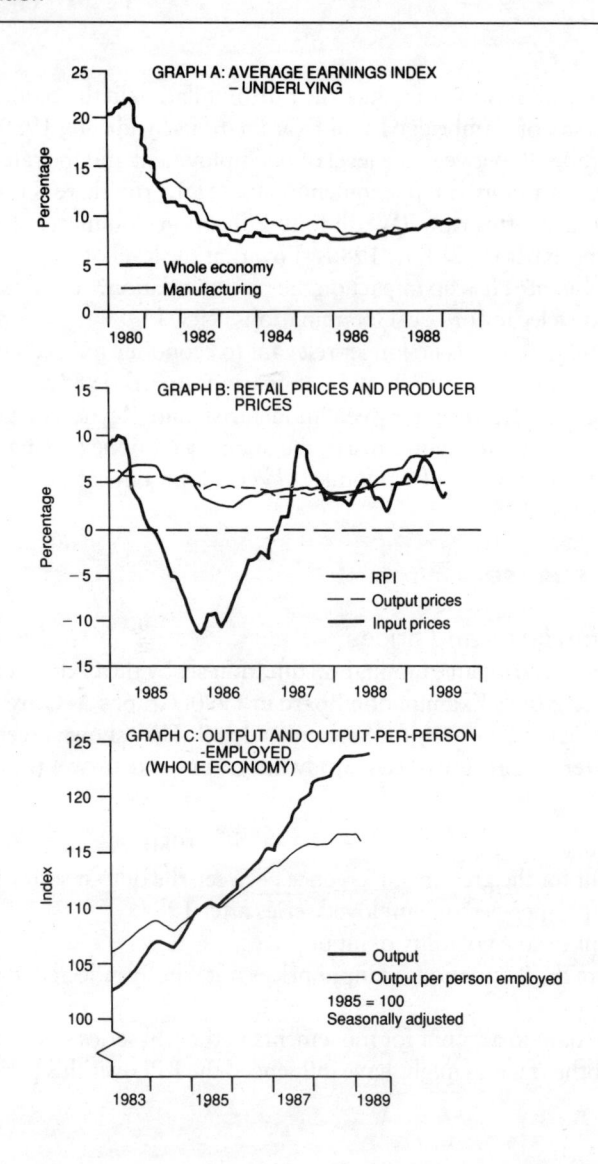

GRAPH A: AVERAGE EARNINGS INDEX – UNDERLYING
- Whole economy
- Manufacturing

GRAPH B: RETAIL PRICES AND PRODUCER PRICES
- RPI
- Output prices
- Input prices

GRAPH C: OUTPUT AND OUTPUT-PER-PERSON-EMPLOYED (WHOLE ECONOMY)
- Output
- Output per person employed

1985 = 100
Seasonally adjusted

Chapter Six
Cost-push inflation

'The first question is, I say, how far it may be possible to fix the rate of wages, irrespectively of the demand for labour.' John Ruskin, Roots of Honour

Market power

Both monetarist and Keynesian explanations of inflation suggest that producers and workers respond to events beyond their control. In the case of the monetarists it is an increase in money supply, and in the case of the Keynesians it is an increase in aggregate demand. Both may be seen as operating through the demand side of the market. Neither prices nor wages have independent causes but simply respond to market conditions.

In this chapter we look at an alternative view. Wages are determined in labour markets by employers competing among themselves for workers (which keeps wages from falling too low) and workers competing among themselves for jobs (which prevents wages rising too high). Prices are determined in goods markets by sellers competing among themselves for customers (which prevents prices rising too much) and customers competing among themselves for goods (which prevents prices falling too far).

In many markets the degree of competition is insufficient to ensure this balance between suppliers and demanders, and **market power** plays a major role in the determination of wages and prices.

Perhaps the best known example of the influence of market power on prices is that in the market for crude oil. There being only a few big suppliers of oil, it became possible for them to collude rather than compete. Instead of each oil producer negotiating a price per barrel with oil users, the major oil producers and exporters formed themselves into a **cartel** in order to act in concert. This cartel is known as OPEC - the Organisation of Petroleum Exporting Countries - and together they fix a price for oil and present oil users with that price.

Oil is essential to most developed economies, so producers have users over a barrel. They have to pay up or perish. It is also a widely used commodity which, in one way or another, enters into the production of most other commodities. This means that if the price of oil increases then so too will the prices of those commodities which depend on it. Thus there will be a rise in general price level, as there was following the oil price rises of 1974/75 and 1979/80. This is shown in Figure 4 and in Table 8. From both these sources it is abundantly clear that the UK's RPI did indeed leap up immediately after OPEC increased the price of crude oil.

Table 8 Retail price index, 1970 - 91

1970	*1971*	*1972*	*1973*	*1974**	*1975*	*1976*	*1977*
135.5	147.0	159.0	171.3	191.8	230.0	283.7	330.7
1978	*1979 **	*1980*	*1981*	*1982*	*1983*	*1984*	*1985*
363.5	397.4	470.5	531.9	595.7	625.1	657.1	690.1
1986	*1987*	*1988*	*1989*	*1990*	*1991*		
728.3	756.6	781.6	839.9	904.2	985.2		

* Indicates oil price hikes

Trade unions

The second-best known example of imperfect markets is the unionized sector of the labour market. **Trades unions** have many purposes - encouraging worker education and safety at work, negotiating hours of work and holiday periods, and supporting legislation which benefits workers - but an important aspect of their work is wage negotiations. Instead of each worker striking a bargain with an employer, a trade union negotiates for all its members together. Presenting a common front confers market power to workers, and so employers have to pay up or do without unionized labour altogether. Since labour, like oil, is a widely used and essential input into all productive enterprises, this increase in wages will force up costs and so force up price level too.

The technical name for the market power being described here is **monopoly power**. Oil producers have the monopoly of oil and trades unions try to have the monopoly of labour. Monopoly power can also reside with the producers of goods and services.

This view of inflation (based on the increasing market power of sellers) is clearly to do with costs increasing even when there is no encouragement to do so from the demand side of the market. It is therefore called 'cost-push inflation'.

Wage differentials

One weakness of the cost-push theory as described so far is that monopoly power may cause price level to be higher than that of a perfectly competitive economy, but it is difficult to see how it can lead to a steady, secular, upward trend in price level. This weakness can be removed if instead of thinking of *the* labour market - as a single market for all kinds of labour - we think of a myriad of labour markets. There will be a market for skilled boilermakers, another for printers and another for bankers etc. Typically each will have its own trade union or professional association which will negotiate for its interests rather than for the interests of all labour.

Once the fragmentation of the labour market is recognized, then the possibility of **wage differentials** is opened up. Different types of labour are ranked in a sort of hierarchy of skills, with the most skilled expecting (and receiving) higher wages and better conditions than those below them in the pecking order. Low-paid groups try to catch up and so use what market power they have to bid for higher wages. If they succeed then those above them in the wage structure use their market power to restore the wage differentials between them and those below them. This then works its way up the hierarchy of skills until the low-wage groups are back (relatively) where they began. These low-wage groups then set out again to raise their wages and the whole process is repeated.

Thus monopoly labour power in a fragmented labour market will lead to a kind of *war of wage differentials*, and this could give rise to a continuing rise of wages - wage inflation. These wage costs have to be passed on, and so prices are forced up too, and then we have cost-induced price inflation.

Income distribution

The idea of wage differentials can be applied in a more general sense. The basic idea is that different income groups fight to maintain or improve their position in the race. It is a question of **income distribution**. Low-paid workers want a bigger slice of the cake, their colleagues want to maintain or improve theirs, and so on. The same is true of those who receive profits. The increase in wage bills would reduce profits and redistribute income (the cake) in favour of labour at the expense of capital. Capitalists are understandably upset by this and seek to restore their income share by increasing the prices of their goods.

On an international level, the role of OPEC members is to redistribute the world 'cake' in their favour. The more they get for their oil the less is available for the workers and capitalists in countries not producing oil.

UK inflation

The cost-push theory of inflation is therefore to do with disagreements about the distribution of national and international income. Different groups, in pursuing mutually incompatible aims, bid up the prices they receive for what they sell. Since their claims jointly exceed the amount available for distribution, prices in general are forced up and will continue upward until agreement is reached, among those with market power, as to a fair and acceptable distribution of income.

Inflation of this kind will of course require the money supply to be increased. As price level increases, so the transactions demand for money will increase, and if this increase in money supply is not forthcoming then it will be necessary to reduce the number of transactions - i.e. reduced output. This will result in less oil being used, less labour being employed and fewer goods being sold.

This is partly what is meant by factors 'pricing themselves out of the market'. Thus if inflation is caused by increasing costs, and if the government fails to increase money supply in line with the inflation rate, then unemployment results.

This is a result which would be predicted by monetarists from Fisher's quantity theory of money, which was discussed on page 33. In the monetarist explanation of inflation, the root cause was an increase in money supply M when output Y and velocity V were constant. According to Fisher's equation this must result in an increase in price level P.

What the cost-push theorists say is that the root cause is cost increases, which lead to price increases. If price level P increases when money supply M and velocity V are constant, then output - and hence employment - must necessarily decrease.

This may seem like poetic justice, in that those who try to take too much of the cake find themselves deprived of cake altogether. However, the world is not quite like that, because those elements of the labour force which have a great deal of market power are able not only to force up their wages, they can also protect themselves from dismissal. The labour which is dismissed is typically that which has little or no market power, and hence little responsibility for the situation and no immunity from it.

Tight money in the face of rising costs will therefore result in higher and higher levels of unemployment. This conjunction of rising costs and prices with high levels of unemployment is what we have elsewhere called stagflation. This cost push account of stagflation does not rely on expectations but rather augments the Phillips curve with sources of cost increases other than those due to excess demand for labour.

KEY WORDS

Market power
Cartel
Trades unions
Monopoly power

Wage differentials
Income distribution
Unemployment
Stagflation

Further reading
Paisley, R. and Quillfeldt, J., Chapter 2 (Metal fatigue), Chapter 7 (Black gold) and Chapter 23 (What about the workers?) in *Economics Investigated*, Collins Educational, 1989.
Trevithick, J.A., Chapter 7 in *Inflation*, Pelican, 1988.

Essay topics
1. Is it meaningful to identify different causes of inflation? (University of London School Examinations Board, 1989)
2. 'Wage increases in excess of increases in productivity inevitably lead to rapidly rising prices and unemployment.' Examine the validity of this statement. (University of London School Examinations Board, 1987)

Data Response

Pay and productivity
This task is based on an examination question set by the Joint Matriculation Board in 1991. Study the two articles and Table A and then answer the following questions.

1. Outline the arguments, as presented in the articles, for and against linking productivity and pay.
2. In the light of economic theory, how would you expect the relationship between productivity and pay to affect the level of employment and the degree of inflation in the economy? What support, if any, for your ideas do you find in Table A?
3. Is it possible to establish principles to ensure that payment to service sector employees is fair and efficient?

No return to a going rate

The recent discussion of pay awards has a depressingly familiar ring. Ford is said to be setting a "going rate" of over 10 per cent which will be followed by others, not only in manufacturing. "Pay explosion," scream the headlines. Ministers urge restraint and warn of the consequences of irresponsibility.

For the best part of 30 years successive governments sought to cajole employers towards a set figure for annual pay rises regardless of whether they had been earned or not. The result was a low-pay, low-productivity economy slipping inexorably down the league table of international competitiveness. The norm became an entitlement.

Only since the trading sector broke free of the going-rate mentality have we started to regain international competitiveness. Employers are constantly balancing the need to pay no more - and no less - than is required to attract and keep the necessary skills and commitment against the need to remain cost-competitive.

With the price of manufactured goods in the shops rising by around 4 per cent per year, it is clear that such a balance can be achieved only with improved performance. Since 1980, manufacturing productivity in Britain has risen by some 60 per cent overall, though with widely varying performances. The CBI's Pay Databank shows that employers expect to achieve further substantial improvements, on average of about 6 per cent, this year.

CBI data show that during the first half of the 1980s at least two-thirds of all firms linked pay to productivity, and the trend has continued since. Employment has risen to record levels, and, according to a recent consumer survey, there has been a perceived improvement in the quality of British-made goods. Export revenues (excluding oil) have been particularly buoyant; Britain's share of world manufactured exports is now rising, probably for the first time this century. It is not generally recognized that we export more, per head of population, than Japan.

All this shows what can be achieved when employers are free to build pay structures that suit their circumstances, and to pursue wage settlements that are financed by real improvements in performance. And at least one manufacturer in three is still achieving productivity improvements that outstrip the corresponding pay settlements.

To say this is not to underestimate the difficulties of maintaining progress towards an internationally competitive manufacturing base, which holds the key to redressing our balance of payments deficit and curbing inflation. With poorer prospects for growth in the domestic market, manufacturers are having to redouble their export efforts to cover investment costs under a high interest rate regime. Since mid-1988, when interest rates took off, employers have also been grappling with inflationary pressures on pay.

Despite the improvement, the link between pay and performance is still not strong enough to ensure that in all cases unit labour costs fall year by year, as they must in a competitive world. If they do not, the result will be fewer jobs. That is why the CBI emphasizes that pay rises must always be linked to improved productivity. There can be only one going rate. It is for unit labour costs. And our international competitors have ensured that it must be negative.

John Banham
Source: *The Times*,
18 January 1990

© Times Newspapers Ltd, 1990

Table A UK manufacturing industry (1985 = 100)

	Employed labour force	Output per person employed	Average weekly earnings per head	Index of retail prices
1982	107.0	84.7	77.4	85.9
1983	102.1	91.8	84.4	89.8
1984	100.5	97.1	91.7	94.3
1985	100.0	100.0	100.0	100.0
1986	97.9	103.1	107.7	103.4
1987	97.0	109.9	116.3	107.7
1988	98.5	115.9	126.2	113.0
1989	98.5	121.6	137.2	121.8

CSO Economic Trends, July 1990; *Employment Gazette,* March 1990

The fallacy about productivity and pay

Should workers be paid according to the productivity of their enterprise? According to senior ministers and CBI leaders the answer is Yes. But the standard answer has always been No.

So where do ministers go wrong? They start from the important proposition that to stop inflation, average wages in the economy should rise only as fast as average productivity. They then suppose that an easy way to achieve this would be if pay in each firm grew at the same rate as productivity in the same firm.

But this method is disastrous and doomed to failure. It is not only unfair but grossly inefficient. There are huge differences in productivity growth between sectors, which are mainly due to technological factors and not to the efforts of the workers. Thus some sectors have inherently greater productivity growth than others - with manufacturing generally outstripping services. Since this reflects no special merit among the workers in manufacturing, why should workers in services increasingly fall behind?

The service workers will not, of course, agree to do so, and market forces are on their side. So the chief result will be additional inflationary pressure, as service workers' pay tries to keep pace with manufacturing. This is the fundamental problem behind the ambulance workers' dispute.

The mechanism can be simply illustrated. Suppose productivity grows at 5 per cent a year in "manufacturing" and 1 per cent in "services" - an average of, say, 3 per cent. If all workers get 3 per cent wage increases, all will be well. But that is not the current philosophy. Government ministers have told those in "manufacturing" that they can reasonably expect more. But then the "service" workers also insist on getting more too. The result is disastrous.

An important reason for our present problems is this half-baked philosophy. Yet these issues are not new. In 1967 William Baumol wrote a famous article in which he explained how economic progress proceeds in a properly functioning economy. Productivity grows faster in manufacturing than in services. But wages grow at the same rate (so that the relative price of manufactures falls).

In this way the fruits of high productivity growth are spread evenly across the economy, not hogged by one group of workers. Thus barbers are four times richer than they were half a century ago because of productivity increases in the rest of the economy. How on earth could anybody believe that efficiency or equity required otherwise?

The inefficiency in productivity-based pay is manifest. If firms with high productivity growth pay higher wages, rather than cutting their prices, their sales will be depressed. Employment in the most productive sectors will be held back, and the least productive sectors (paying lower wages) will continue to waste labour. In international competition the country will be increasingly forced to specialise in low-productivity, low-wage industries.

This is the opposite of what would happen in a proper competitive labour market. Under competition, workers of a given type would be paid the same regardless of who employed them. And this would ensure that as a nation we best exploited our international comparative advantage.

Richard Layard
Source: *Financial Times*, 31 January 1990

Chapter Seven
Expectations

'In general however a change in circumstances or expectations will cause some realignment in individual holdings of money.' John Maynard Keynes, *The General Theory*

Introduction
In economics we try to explain behaviour in terms of how economic agents respond to certain stimuli such as price changes and income changes. No doubt there is much to be explained in this way, but in many cases the decisions we make today depend on what we think the future will be like. If we are thinking of buying a computer we certainly look at its price and are aware of how much we can afford to spend, but we are also conscious of the fact that computer design is ever improving. Should we buy now and risk being out of date (superseded) in a year's time, or should we wait for the next generation of computers? Producers, too, when deciding whether to build a new plant, must consider what the future demand for their products will be. The future is a closed book to us and we have to wait a day before another page of time is revealed. Thus we are in something of an impasse: we cannot act without knowing the future and we cannot know the future. What we do in such circumstances is to guess what the future will be and act accordingly. In other words, we base current actions on what we *expect* the future to look like.

Official forecasters try to take account of our **expectations** and, more broadly, our 'confidence' in their prognostications. The Bank of England refers to the **index of consumer confidence** shown in Figure 12 thus:

> 'Adding further support to the view that recent upturns in retail sales and consumption may prove erratic is the EC/Gallup indicator of consumer confidence, which has followed a downward path since policy started to tighten in mid-1988 and is currently lower than at the depth of the 1981-82 recession.' (*Bank of England Quarterly Bulletin*, May 1990)

In this chapter we examine how we might form our expectations and how those expectations affect our behaviour.

Expectations

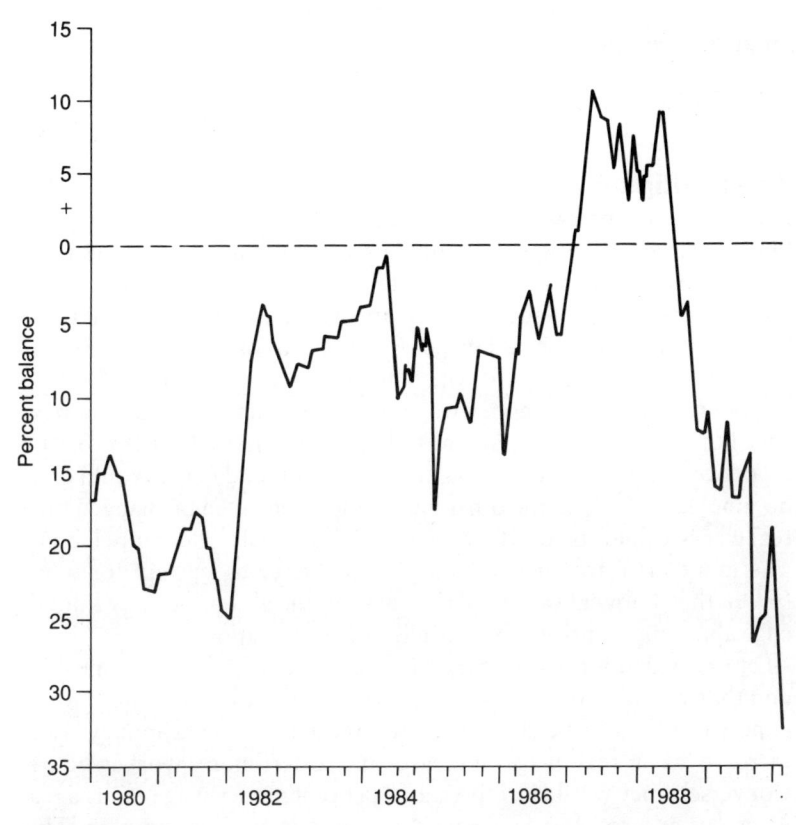

Figure 12 Consumer confidence (the EC/Gallup indicator)

Regressive expectations

Keynes was well aware of the role of expectations and devoted two chapters of *The General Theory* to them. He argued that they had an appreciable effect, that they were subject to wide fluctuations and that, in forming them, we begin by looking back at what happened in the past:

> 'Accordingly it is sensible for producers to base their expectations on the assumption that the most recently realised results will continue, except in so far as there are definite reasons for expecting a change.'

It is this tendency for us to look backwards in order to know the future which leads to the word **regressive**.

In many walks of life this method of forming expectations works quite well. Today's weather is a good indicator of tomorrow's. If we know someone who has been quiet and reasonable all his life we will act as if he will continue to be quiet and reasonable. Similarly for economics; if output has been increasing at 2 per cent a year for 20 years, then we will expect it to grow by 2 per cent next year too. Unless of course, as Keynes said, we have reason to believe otherwise - e.g. because of a war.

The Phillips curve

In an earlier chapter we came across expectations when discussing the **Phillips curve**. The original Phillips curve showed a stable relationship between unemployment and the rate of change of money wage rate. This, according to the monetarists, arose because workers took these money wage rises to be real wage rises and thus offered more worker-hours (lower unemployment) when money wage rates rose.

They knew that their money wages were going up by 10 per cent next year but did not know what was to happen to prices. If prices rose by 10 per cent too then they would be no better off and hence would offer no more labour. If, on the other hand, prices remained unchanged then real wages would rise by 10 per cent and they would offer more labour. The monetarist argument is that workers have to sign up for work *before* they know about price rises and, in the absence of any knowledge about future prices, they would form expectations.

Let us say that for many years there had been no inflation to speak of and that workers formed their expectations regressively. They would expect inflation to be zero and interpret a 10 per cent money wage increase as a real wage increase and offer more worker-hours. Conversely they would interpret a 10 per cent money wage cut as a real wage cut and so offer fewer worker-hours in the coming year. This would trace out the relationship between changes in money wage rates and unemployment found by Phillips.

As we have seen, these money wage increases must lead to inflation if they exceed labour productivity increases. Thus workers will eventually experience rising prices and slowly begin to revise their expectations. If they expect prices to rise by 10 per cent next year then they will want 10 per cent more money wages just to keep employment at today's level. Thus the whole Phillips curve moves upwards by 10 per cent or by whatever the expected inflation rate is.

With the expected inflation rate of 10 per cent, workers will interpret a money wage rate increase of 20 per cent as a 10 per cent increase in real wage rate, and so offer more workers. This 20 per cent wage increase will lead to higher inflation, which will eventually be seen by the workers and so expectations will be revised upwards too.

The natural rate or NAIRU

The point is that workers can be persuaded to depart from their normal

Expectations

employment level only when they are mistaken in their expectations. When they over-predict inflation they offer too little and when they under-predict inflation they offer too much.

The level of unemployment at which there are no mistaken expectations is called the **natural rate of unemployment** - this was shown in Figure 11 on page 51.

When workers expect inflation to be zero the natural rate occurs with an actual inflation rate of zero. When workers expect inflation to be 10 per cent then the natural rate occurs with an actual inflation rate of 10 per cent. And when workers expect inflation to be minus 5 per cent then the natural rate occurs with an actual inflation rate of minus 5 per cent. Any attempt to drive unemployment below the natural rate requires wage increases greater than the expected inflation rate and hence must increase the actual inflation rate. Any attempt to drive unemployment above its natural rate requires a money wage increase of less than the expected inflation rate and hence will bring about a fall in the inflation rate. Thus all unemployment rates below the natural rate lead to a steadily increasing rate of inflation – this is called **accelerating inflation**. Similarly, all unemployment rates above the natural rate lead to a steadily falling inflation rate. Keeping unemployment at its natural rate keeps inflation at its constant, expected rate. Thus another name for the natural rate of unemployment is the *non-accelerating inflation rate of unemployment,* or **NAIRU**.

According to this theory, then, the level of inflation is determined by what we *expect* it to be and how far above or below the natural rate of unemployment we are.

Of these two influences (expectations and the level of demand) expectations is the more powerful. Reducing people's expectations of inflation from 15 to 10 per cent immediately reduces actual inflation by 5 per cent with no increases in the unemployment rate. It seems reasonable, therefore, to try to control inflation by operating on expectations rather than on aggregate demand. Basically this means moving the whole Phillips curve downwards rather than moving along it.

Catch 22

The separation of demand management on the one hand from manipulating expectations on the other is not as complete as might appear. If expectations are formed regressively (by looking at what has happened in the recent past) then the only way to change expectations is to change what is actually happening. This is something of a 'Catch 22' - to reduce inflation we must first reduce expected inflation; to reduce expected inflation we must first reduce actual inflation.

The outcome is a return to demand management with the additional element that, by reducing aggregate demand, we not only move *along* the Phillips curve, we *move it downwards* as expectations are reduced. This is bad news.

Gradualism

The shape of the curve is such that to the right of the NAIRU the slope is shallow but to the left it is quite steep. Thus, to reduce inflation by 10 per cent it is necessary to impose huge unemployment levels, and this can be quickly undone by a brief excursion to the left of NAIRU where a 10 per cent increase will occur with a small level of over-employment.

The dilemma facing the policy-makers is whether to impose massive increases in unemployment to quickly reduce inflation and inflationary expectations, or whether to impose slight increases in unemployment and slowly reduce expectations. In either case, when expectations have been reduced to zero, unemployment can be allowed to return to its natural (NAIRU) rate.

Some argue for a short, sharp shock. Others prefer the softly, softly, approach and this difference in opinion is reflected in policy debates.

Rational expectations

The dilemma outlined above arose because expectations could be affected only by changing the actual level of inflation, but there are other views about our expectation-forming process. The most recent - and certainly the most influential - of these alternative views argues that agents have a great deal of information about how the economy is going and it would be foolish of them to ignore all this when thinking about inflation. When agents take into account all the relevant economic theory and information when forming their expectations, they are said to form **rational expectations**.

Cobwebs

The basic idea of rational expectations sprang from economists' dissatisfaction with some of the consequences of assuming regressive (backward-looking) expectations. This is most powerfully demonstrated by the inability of some markets to find an equilibrium with regressive expectations. Consider a market for pigs. The demand for pigs depends on the current price of pigs - as price rises so the demand falls. The supply of pigs today depends on how many were bred one year ago, if it takes about a year to fatten them from piglets to porkers. The number of pigs bred a year ago clearly depends on the price the breeder *expects* to get for them when they are brought to market in one year's time.

Expectations

With regressive expectations tomorrow's price is expected to be the same as today's price. So, current supply depends on (increases with) last year's price and demand decreases with current price. This is shown in Figure 13.

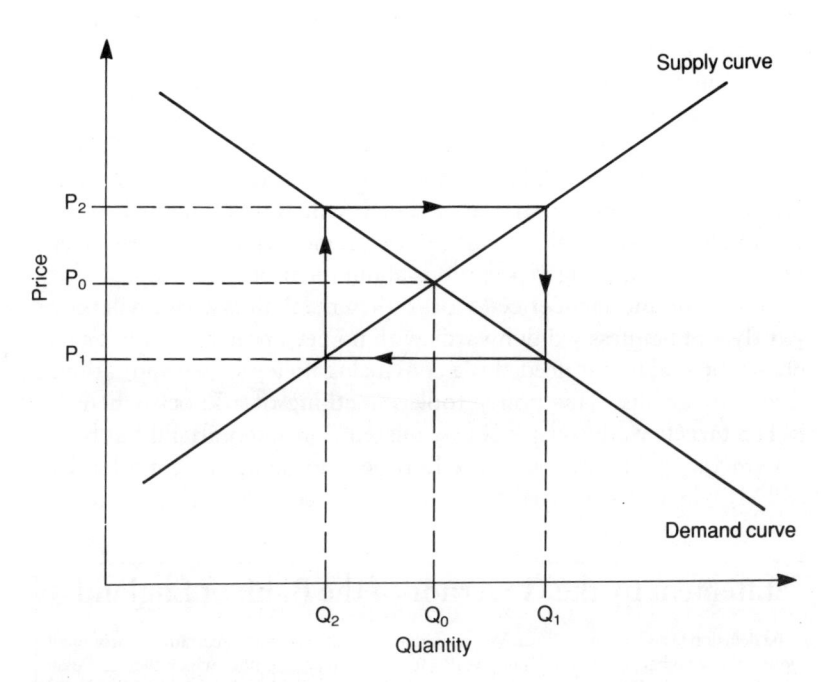

Figure 13 The cobweb

If we start off with supply Q_1 then price will be determined by the demand curve and will be P_1. At price P_1 breeders will cut supply to Q_2, and so next year, when Q_2 come on to the market, the price will rise to P_2. But at this price, supply will return to Q_1 and so price will return to P_1 and the cycle will start all over again.

Price and output in this market (the hog market) continue to fluctuate and never settle down to the equilibrium of P_0 and Q_0. This is called the **cobweb model**.

Now no rational economic agent is going to watch this cycle of prices and continue to form expectations regressively – sooner or later the way the market is working would become apparent and expectations would be formed in accordance with the relevant economic theory. That is what rational expectations are.

The rational expectations model has been enthusiastically embraced by monetarists, and they argue that agents understand enough economic theory to know that inflation depends on money supply. In forming their expectations about inflation they therefore try to predict what will happen to money supply, and hence will listen to the government's declared monetary policy. This is what gives the government power to influence inflation simply by announcing an intention to control money supply.

For this policy to be effective, announcements must be convincing, and recent governments have put a great deal of effort into this aspect of their anti-inflation policy. There have been informal announcements, such as 'No U-turn', 'The lady is not for turning', and 'There is no alternative' (Tina). A formal form first made its appearance in the **medium-term financial strategy** (MTFS) which was designed to pre-commit the government to a future strict money regime and give a clear signal to those forming expectations about inflation.

If the **'announcement effect'** works, then the Phillips curve will move swiftly and painlessly downwards with no need to enforce any unemployment – all that is needed is a convincing policy stance and rational economic agents. This policy took something of a knock when the MTFS targets were conspicuously missed. The latest attempt at being convincing is our entry into the European **exchange rate mechanism** (ERM) which is supposed to reinforce our commitment to reducing money supply growth.

Statement by the Governor of the Bank of England

The decision last October to join the exchange rate mechanism of the European monetary system can be seen in this light. It reinforces our anti-inflationary policy through the public acceptance of the discipline embodied in the obligation to keep sterling within fixed bands against other ERM currencies. In this way, the ERM provides a clear framework for monetary policy; and it provides an external discipline on policy-makers. The flexibility we have as policy-makers depends on the performance of sterling in the band; and this, in turn, depends on the credibility and consistency of our policies. For businesses, the ERM offers a more certain environment within which they can plan investment decisions and identify more clearly than in the past the constraints about product pricing and pay settlements. Once again, this requires consistency and resolve from policy-makers. No-one should have any doubt about that resolve.

The beauty of this direct attack on inflationary expectations is that it avoids the need to impose high levels of unemployment - it is a painless way of returning to zero inflation. But if workers are not convinced by all this and continue to bargain as if inflation were to remain at 15 per cent, then it will be necessary to increase unemployment. The blame for this would be placed squarely at the door of the workers themselves for not being rational.

> **KEY WORDS**
>
> Expectations
> Index of consumer confidence
> Regressive
> Phillips curve
> Natural rate of unemployment
> Accelerating inflation
> NAIRU
> Rational expectations
> Cobweb model
> Medium-term financial strategy
> Announcement effect
> Exchange rate mechanism

Further reading
Healey, N and Parker, D., Chapter 7 in Current Topics in *Economic Theory*, Anforme, 1990.
Levačić, R., *Supply Side Economics*, Heinemann Educational, 1988.
Pennant-Rea, Chapter 5 in *The Economist Economics*, Penguin, 1986.
Robinson, B., 'Monetary growth and inflation', *Economic Review*, Jan. 1991.
Sumner, M., 'The Phillips curve', *Economic Review*, May 1984.

Essay topics
1. How are wages determined in the United Kingdom? Discuss whether the methods of wage determination are a cause of current economic problems. (Associated Examining Board, 1988).
2. 'In the fight against inflation it is as important to control inflationary expectations as it is to control money supply'. Discuss. (Associated Examining Board, 1991).

Chapter Eight
Economic policies

'The control of inflation is the judge and the jury of a government's economic policy.' Nigel Lawson (when Chancellor of the Exchequer)

Immediately following the Second World War the Labour government was preoccupied with finding jobs and housing for all those released from war production and from the armed forces, and with earning foreign exchange – particularly US dollars. Government control and central planning were still strong and there was little desire to embrace fully the free-market approach of pre-war days. Monetary policy in particular was very lax, and the Chancellor pursued a 'cheap money' policy perfectly in line with the Keynesian view that money did not really matter.

The story over the last 40 years has been one of a steady movement away from planning controls and 'cheap money' of the Keynesians towards the free-market 'tight money' policies of the monetarists. There are now signs of disillusionment with modern monetarism. Policy it seems is always on the move.

In this chapter we shall trace through this ever-changing landscape of policy and find that some landmarks seem to recur.

Prices and incomes policies

We have already seen that the Keynesian explanation of inflation rested on there being too much aggregate demand in the presence of certain bottlenecks in supply. If the control of aggregate demand, via fiscal policy, went beyond full-employment level, then there would be an inflationary gap and prices, rather than employment, would begin to increase.

Empirical work by Phillips showed that there was no single point at which the effect of expanding aggregate demand would suddenly change from employment-enhancing to price inflation. He showed that as demand expanded at first, with high unemployment rates, employment changed a lot and price level changed only a little. However, as demand was further expanded the changes in employment would be less pronounced and those of price level more apparent.

This work of Phillips and his followers had a profound effect on economic policy. The Phillips curve told policy-makers that they could either have low inflation and high unemployment or low unemployment and high inflation – they could not have both low inflation and low unemployment.

Given this 'trade-off' between two of the things the government wanted, it was up to the politicians to decide what combination of inflation and unemployment they preferred; they then operated on aggregate demand until they reached their preferred point on the Phillips curve. If they chose a high-unemployment/low-inflation combination, labour unions would complain. If they chose low-unemployment/high-inflation, consumers and exporters would complain. It is simply not possible to please all the people all the time.

In order to ease their dilemma the government set out to alter the shape of the Phillips curve. Its shape was determined by the tendency for wage bargainers to press for higher and higher wage increases when the demand for goods (and hence the demand for workers) exceeded supply. This excess demand makes it possible for producers to increase wages and to cover these cost increases by increasing the prices of their goods.

The fact that these things are possible does not imply that they are necessary. Human behaviour is not governed by the immutable laws of physics but is a matter of free choice of free wills. Thus, although in the past we may have responded to excess demand by increasing wages and prices, we need not continue doing so – things could be otherwise. It is in this sense that the government can try to change the shape of the Phillips curve. They tried to persuade workers not to take advantage of labour shortages by pushing up wages and to persuade producers not to take advantage of excess demand for their goods by putting up prices.

This formed the basis of the various prices and incomes policies (called the **Social Contract** by Harold Wilson) tried at various times in the sixties and seventies. The 'contract', between the government and labour on the one hand and between the government and producers on the other hand, was that the government would increase aggregate demand so as to keep unemployment down to very low levels provided that no-one took advantage of the high level of demand to increase wages or prices.

This policy was sometimes merely a voluntary code of behaviour which was more honoured in the breach than in the observance, and at times there were statutory prices and incomes policies under which wage rates and prices were constrained by law or at least backed up by some sanctions.

These too met with little success. One reason was that relative prices must be allowed to change if the price mechanism is to work properly, and it is difficult to change relative prices when prices are being controlled. Second, when the policy was eventually taken off there was a sudden, sharp rise in both wages and prices which undid effects of the policy in the first place.

The effectiveness of incomes policies may be summed up as follows:

> '. . . whilst some incomes policies have reduced the rate of wage inflation during the period in which they operated, this reduction has only been temporary. Wage increases in the period immediately following the ending of policies were higher . . . and these increases match losses incurred during the operation of the incomes policy.'
>
> (Henry and Ormerod, *National Institute Economic Review*, Aug 1978; quoted by Vane and Thompson, *Macro Economic Policy*, Harvester Press, 1982)

Credit controls

Throughout this period the dominant theory put almost all the emphasis on controlling aggregate demand through fiscal policy, and discounted monetary policy – what happened to money supply was simply a side-effect of fiscal decisions. But some attention was paid to controlling credit. Typically this control was exercised on the credit households used for buying consumer durables. The controls were of two forms. First, there had to be some proportion of the loan already saved by the borrower – the so-called 'down-payment'. To borrow £100 it was necessary to already have, say, £10 or £30 to pay towards the good. The exact proportion depended on how tight the restriction was. Second, the period over which the loan had to be repaid was also controlled. The shorter the repayment period and the higher the down-payment, the less attractive the borrowing would be.

Credit controls are still occasionally discussed but are nowadays seen as an unwarranted intrusion by the government into our economic affairs. Towards the end of the last Labour government the Chancellor sought the help of the International Monetary Fund (the IMF) to prop up the international value of the pound – the exchange rate. A condition attached to this deal was that the UK should pay more attention to money supply and rein in public expenditure – i.e. switch the emphasis from fiscal to monetary policy. The feeling was, however, that this switch was only reluctantly accepted, because the government's heart was still with fiscal policy.

Soon afterwards the Conservative party won the 1979 election and abandoned Keynesian policies as a matter of theoretical conviction rather than as a reluctant client of the IMF. The move was towards balanced budgets and tight money.

Monetarist policies

As we saw in Chapter 4, monetarists hold that inflation is always and everywhere a monetary phenomenon. Milton Friedman in particular absolves labour from any responsibility for inflation since labour is unable to control money supply. Thus when Mrs Thatcher's administration came to power the whole emphasis of anti-inflation policy switched from controlling markets to controlling money supply. The first step of any such policy is to identify what constitutes money in our economy and who issues it.

Money

So far we have defined money as the medium of exchange, and it is increases in the medium of exchange which monetarists blame for inflation. We have kept to a very simple idea of media of exchange – coins and notes supplied by the state – but in a modern economy this will not do. Coins and notes are indeed used as a medium of exchange but only for relatively small transactions. For larger transactions, and by far the greater value of all transactions, cheques and credit cards are used, and these are not supplied by the government but by the commercial banks, building societies, shops etc.

In other words, there are many media of exchange supplied by various sources and more are being added to the list as time passes. It is clearly important for monetarists to have a clear idea of what we use as money and what determines its supply. There being no single medium of exchange the government defines (and from time to time redefines) various categories of media of exchange.

The first, and most basic, medium of exchange is *cash* which consists of notes and coin. Cash is *legal tender*, which means that it must be accepted as payment, and it is exclusively supplied by the government. Not all the notes and coins in existence are always in circulation with the public. Some are held in the tills of banks and some are deposited by banks in the Bank of England. All notes and coin, wherever held, officially constitute a 'narrow' definition of our money; this is called M0.

The second type of medium of exchange is our access to cheques. The amounts we hold in chequing accounts determine how many cheques we can write. Although they are not legal tender (sellers need not accept cheques), by and large cheques drawn on a commercial bank will be accepted by most sellers.

Many banks now allow cheques to be drawn on deposit accounts as well as chequing accounts, and if the sums held in those accounts are denominated in sterling then they too will constitute part of our medium of exchange. Building societies also provide us with chequing accounts, and these too are part of our medium of exchange. All these taken together with foreign currency bank and building society deposits constitute a 'broad' measure of money supply; this is called **M4**.

There are many more types of 'money', and definitions have changed greatly over time. They have been variously named from M1 through to M5, passing through PSL1 and PSL2 on the way. The PSLs were measures of 'public sector liquidity' in exactly the same way as the Ms were – only the names were changed. These six measures have the property that the higher the number the broader the definition. That is all we really need to know about types of money.

This tendency for our definition of 'money' to change presents economists and politicians with enormous problems – particularly those seeking to prove or to use a relationship between money supply and inflation.

Monetary policy

The Chancellor of the Exchequer in the first Thatcher administration (Sir Geoffrey Howe) spelt out monetarist policy in a budget statement in 1979:

> 'We are committed to the progressive reduction of the rate of growth of the money supply.'

By **money supply** he meant £M3 (sterling M3) and the annual growth rate was to be between 7 and 11 per cent.

This was followed one year later by the advent of the **medium-term financial strategy** (MTFS) which set targets for money supply and the public sector borrowing requirement (**PSBR**) from 1980 to 1984. Annual increases in money supply were to be reduced from 7–11 to 4–8 per cent over that period. This pre-commitment of a four-year programme of slowing down the rate of change of money supply was to have two effects. First, its eventual implementation would reduce annual inflation rates according to the monetarist theory. Second, since everyone was to know what money supply – and hence inflation – would be in the medium term, they would avoid mistakes due to erroneous expectations of inflation. This second effect depends largely on how convincing the government is. If we all believe that they will actually meet the medium term financial strategy, then we will form our expectations accordingly; but if we doubt the commitment to the policy or the government's ability to carry it out, then we will form expectations as we always do – mistakenly.

Thus the government tries to be convincing when it announces the MTFS.

Table 9 The results of monetary targetry (successful outcomes are marked with an asterisk)

Year targeted	\multicolumn{8}{c}{Year of publication of FSBR (March), percentage increases}	Outcome		Overshoot over top end of range	
	1979	1980	1981	1982	1983	1984	1985	1986				

£M3
1978–79	8–12											
1979–80	7–11								16.2		5.2	
1980–81		7–11							18.4		7.4	
1981–82		6–10	6–10						12.8		2.8	
1982–83		5–9	5–9	8–12					11.1*		0.0	
1983–84		4–8	4–8	7–11	7–11				9.5*		0.0	
1984–85				6–10	6–10	6–10			11.9		1.9	
1985–86					5–9	5–9	5–9		16.3		7.3	
1986–87						4–8	4–8		18.7		3.7	
1987–88						3–7	3–7				28.3	
1988–89						2–6	2–6	11–15			=31.1%	

M1 and PSL2
									M1	PSL2	M1	PSL2
1982–83				8–12					12.3	11.5*	0.3	0.0
1983–84				7–11	7–11				14.0	12.4	3.0	1.4
1984–85				6–10	6–10						3.3	1.4
1985–86					5–9						=14.3%	=6.1%

Notes: £M3 was renamed M3 in May 1987 and no longer published from June 1989. PSL2 was renamed M5 in May 1987, and from 1982 onwards only the next year's figure was a target; those for subsequent years became 'illustrative ranges'.

Sources: *Financial Statement and Budget Report; Financial Statistics*, Bank of England

Unfortunately the outturn was somewhat different from the target, and by 1980 £M3 was growing at 18 per cent a year. This led, not to the revision of targets, but to a change in what was being targeted. £M3, PSL2 (now called M5) and M1 were all targeted and were to be between 8 and 12 per cent. This proved more successful (see Table 9); but subsequent changes in targets, the wide ranges of the target areas and the failure often to achieve even these target ranges suggest to the uncommitted observer that the government is unable to control money supply however one cares to define it. If that is so, then monetarism is called into question.

Interest rate policy

Part of the problem faced by the government in controlling the supply of money lies in the fact that the bulk of money supply is provided by the banking sector rather than the government. The banks allow customers to swell the sums in their chequing accounts by offering them overdrafts, and this means we have more medium of exchange. It used to be the case that the government could limit the creation of **bank credit** by insisting that the credit they extended was always backed by a certain amount of cash. This meant that before a bank could increase its lending (create more overdrafts) it first had to increase its holding of cash (in tills or as deposits at the Bank of England). Since the government controlled the amount of cash in the economy it could also control the amount in chequing accounts. This broke down when the regulations governing the behaviour of banks underwent successive and radical changes. The control over the expansion of chequing accounts was greatly weakened in 1980 when banks were no longer required to keep meaningful cash or liquid asset ratios. Control over money supply was certainly too weak to articulate a strict monetary policy.

The huge increase in household debt can be seen from Figure 14. It was about 40 per cent of household income up to 1980 and thereafter gradually climbed to 100 per cent. The boom in house prices provided the collateral for those demanding loans, and the banks, being released from constraints, could provide the loans. Some of the borrowing went on house purchase, which further pushed up house prices and so provided even more collateral for borrowers – an upward credit spiral unaffected by monetary policy. This failure to control the credit creation by the commercial banks – and hence the failure to control money supply – led to a shift in policy away from the supply side to the demand side. Banks can offer us more and more overdrafts but they cannot make us accept them. Thus they supply but do we demand?

The cost to us of taking an overdraft is the interest charged, and so as interest rates increase so our willingness to become more indebted to the banks is decreased. This relationship between interest rate and money supply is shown in Figure 15.

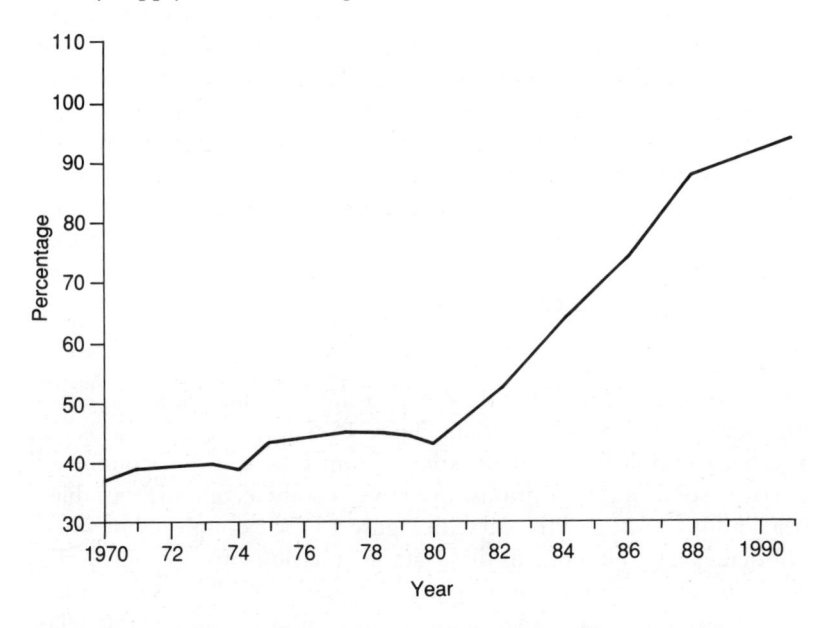

Figure 14 Household debt as a percentage of household income

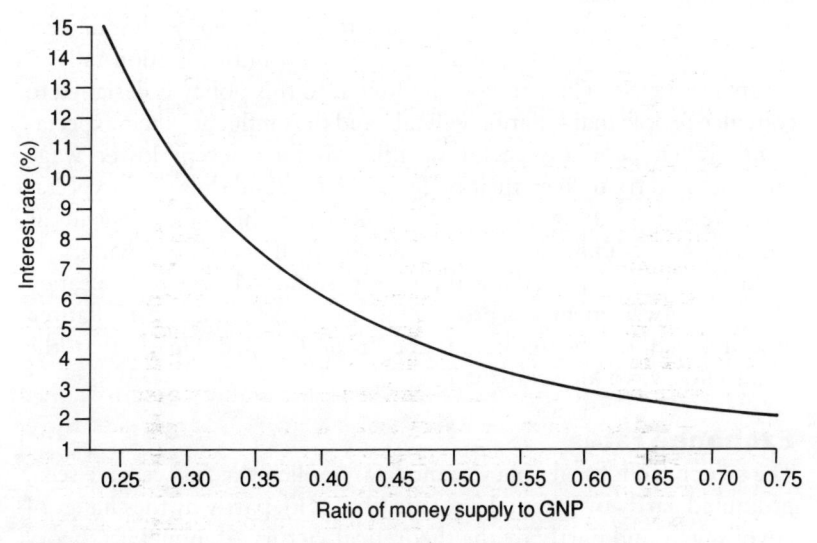

Figure 15 Interest rates and the demand for money

UK inflation

In that figure the horizontal axis is the ratio of money to GNP (gross national product). This ratio, rather than simply the supply of money, is used since the **demand for money**, as we saw earlier, depends on the number of transactions (measured by output). Thus the graph shows how the quantity of money *per transaction* changes as interest rate changes. It is clear from this graph that, for any given level of GNP (i.e. if we hold the number of transactions constant) the demand for money falls as interest rate rises.

The government therefore instituted a regime of high interest rates (which they do claim to have control over) in the hope that banks would be unable to issue any more credit and might even have to take back some of the credit already issued.

Goodhart's law

There is some evidence that the credit crunch is being felt and is hurting, but the reduction is less than Figure 15 would suggest. This is yet another example of Goodhart's law. From time to time economists uncover some stable relationship between some economic variables (the Phillips curve and the curve in Figure 15 are examples), but when politicians try to use one of these 'stable' relationships to control the economy then that relationship breaks down – Goodhart's law. Such policies are therefore always on the move looking for new stable relationships.

Expectations again

The high interest rate policy continues to be pursued, with ministers reiterating their determination not to ease up until inflation falls to acceptable levels. The strong commitment to this policy is designed to convince people that inflation will fall, and thus influence their expectations. When people expect low inflation they accept lower wage increases and try to keep their prices down too, and thus their expectations are self-fulfilling. In a sense the success of this policy depends as much on its **credibility** as on its real power to influence borrowing.

The interest rate policy was thought by some to be the only weapon which the government was prepared to use in its fight against inflation, and this led to the (golfers') jibe from Edward Heath that the Chancellor was a 'one club man'.

Exchange rates

The switch from fiscal policy to monetary policy was, as we have seen, prompted partly by external pressure (the IMF), partly by the change of government and partly by the theoretical victory of monetary theory over Keynesianism. But there was another reason for this switch. Fiscal policy works well under fixed exchange rate regimes but is weak when exchange rates are allowed to float. The converse is true of monetary policy. In June 1972 we allowed the pound to float and thus perforce we adopted monetary policies.

There is some disagreement about the freedom of our exchange rate during the following years, with official policy being that the market would determine exchange rates but intervention by the authorities from time to time suggested that the government had a view about its preferred level and would seek to influence it.

During Nigel Lawson's chancellorship it was thought that he tried to keep the value of the pound in line with that of Germany's mark – i.e. he shadowed the deutschmark – at about 3DM to the pound in 1990.

In order to do this, of course, our inflation rate must, in the long run, be in line with Germany's rate. When the exchange rate rather than money supply is being targeted, the role of interest rate manipulation takes on an additional aspect. The UK exchange rates tend to rise when the international demand for pounds exceeds the supply of pounds. It tends to fall when supply exceeds demand. The demand for pounds depends on two things.

First, foreigners demand pounds when they wish to buy UK goods and services. We supply pounds (demand marks) when we wish to buy German goods and services. Thus if our imports of German goods and services exceed Germany's demand for our goods and services, the pound will fall against the mark. This is called the **current account surplus** (or deficit) and is improved when our inflation rate is low – i.e. when our economy is depressed by high interest rates.

Second, foreigners' demand for pounds depends on their demand for our bonds and shares (financial assets). If UK interest rates rise above German interest rates, Germans will prefer UK bonds to German bonds and so will demand pounds with which to buy the UK bonds. This is called the **capital account surplus** (or deficit).

Therefore, increasing UK interest rates will tend to reduce our inflation *and* increase our exchange rate too.

Interest rate policy is therefore suitable for both inflation and exchange rate targeting, and hence the Chancellor could be implicitly shadowing the mark whilst claiming to achieve the targets of the MTFS.

The ERM
This shadowing of the deutschmark became more explicit on our decision to enter the **exchange rate mechanism**. Essentially this is a fixed

exchange rate regime in which the exchange rate of the pound for other European currencies is held within a band (currently ±6 per cent) around a fixed rate. The significance of this is two-fold.

First, in a fixed exchange rate system any inflation will reduce international competitiveness so that excessive wage or price increases will lead to loss of orders, unemployment and idle factories. In other words, it is an externally imposed discipline on wage and price fixers.

Second, by committing itself to a fixed exchange rate the government increases the credibility of its anti-inflation stance. It simply cannot maintain a fixed exchange rate if it issues (or allows to be issued) too much money. This is tantamount to saying that the government can either have a monetary policy or an exchange rate policy but not both. It is partly for this reason that the more committed monetarists, like Sir Alan Walters and Mrs Thatcher, were so reluctant to enter the ERM – it meant giving up 'discretionary action to control UK money supply' (i.e. giving up monetary policy). The only escape open to them would be to set money supply and 'devalue' (i.e. to lower the fixed rate around which the 6 per cent is allowed) if that proved too much. In order to stop up that hole, both the government and the Governor of the Bank of England have been emphatic in rejecting any such move. Thus we are strongly committed to low inflation.

A commitment to a **common currency** throughout Europe is tantamount to a completely fixed exchange rate and is viewed with alarm by those who remain committed to monetary policy. Were we to adopt a common currency we would have no monetary policy and would have to fall back on fiscal measures for all internal economic control.

Fiscal policy

Throughout successive Conservative administrations, fiscal policy has simply been to reduce the public sector borrowing requirement and reduce tax rates. If the government can neither borrow nor raise taxes, it follows that it must cut expenditure or raise funds by 'selling off the family silver', and this has been a hallmark of successive budget proposals. If cuts in central government expenditure are more than matched by increased spending by the private sector, then fiscal policy will boost demand. This was the case when Nigel Lawson was Chancellor in 1988, and he cut the standard rate of income tax at a time when demand was already rising. Thus as far as aggregate demand is concerned, fiscal policy can still be used, but according to monetarists the only way of causing inflation is by increasing the money supply. Thus, with tight money, tax cuts are not inflationary. Despite this article of monetarist faith there seems to linger even in the breasts of committed monetarists the residual feeling that aggregate demand does matter and can be inflationary. It certainly now seems to be the case that aggregate demand is being held down in order to 'squeeze inflation out of the system', and this will continue until actual and expected inflation rates are in line with those in the rest of Europe.

The timing of Chancellor Lawson's tax cuts may have been mistaken. The data on which his decision was based were like all official statistics – late, unreliable and subject to revision. This, coupled with the fact that fiscal and monetary policies take time to work, often leads to policy errors. For this reason some economists (notably Friedman) want to minimise the amount of discretion politicians have in economic matters.

Policy seems to have come almost a full circle in the last 30 years. We began with fixed exchange rates, credit controls and fiscal policy. We moved to control of only money and the reduction of the role of fiscal policy, to balancing the budget and reducing the size of the public sector. This proved too simple a view of inflation and there has been a gradual move back towards a fixed exchange rate and credit controls.

KEY WORDS

Prices and incomes policies
Social Contract
M0
M4
Money supply
Medium-term financial strategy
PSBR
Interest rate policy

Bank credit
Demand for money
Credibility
Capital account surplus
Current account surplus
Exchange rate mechanism
Common currency

Further reading

Healey, N., 'Breaking the mould?' *British Economic Survey*, Longman, Autumn 1989.

Johnson, C., *The Economy Under Mrs Thatcher 1979–1990*, Penguin, 1991

McCrostie, M., 'Money: definition and measurement', *Economic Review*, May 1988.

Reddaway, B., 'Testing monetarist theory', *Economic Review*, Sept. 1989.

Smith, D., Chapter 2 in *Mrs Thatcher's Economics*, 2nd edn, Heinemann Educational, 1992.

Vane, H.R. and Thompson, J.L., Chapter 11 in *An Introduction to Macro Economic Policy*, Harvester Press, 1982.

Essay topics

1. Outline the objectives of monetary policy in the UK in recent years. Discuss the problems that the Bank of England has encountered in operating monetary policy. (University of London School Examinations Board, 1991).
2. Are budget deficits necessarily inflationary? (University of Oxford Delegacy of Local Examinations, 1990)
3. 'British membership of the European exchange rate mechanism is a strategy designed to reduce the rate of inflation at the expense of domestic output and employment'. Discuss. (Oxford & Cambridge Schools Examination Board, 1991)
4. 'The rise in inflation in 1988 was the result of over rapid expansion of the economy'. Do you agree? (Oxford & Cambridge Schools Examination Board, 1989)
5. What is inflation and why is it commonly regarded as a problem? In what ways have anti-inflationary policies changed in Britain over the last two decades? (Joint Matriculation Board, 1991)

Data Response

Economic indicators

This task is based on an examination question set by the Southern Universities Joint Board in 1989. When using economic indicators, economists have to be aware of the nature and quality of the data available to them. Tables A and B, which are produced and updated every month by the Department of Employment, show some important monthly performance indicators for the economy as a whole.

1. What happened to the index of retail prices in January 1987?
2. Suggest two reasons why this change was made.
3. What evidence is there of an increase in the level of inflation over this period?

Economic policies

Table A RPI

Month	All items index (Jan 1974 = 100)	Percentage increase over 12 months
Oct 1986	388.4	3.0
Nov	391.7	3.5
Dec	393.0	3.7
Jan 1987	394.5	3.9
Feb	100.4*	3.9
Mar	100.6	4.0
Apr	101.8	4.2
May	101.9	4.1
June	101.9	4.2
July	101.8	4.4
Aug	102.1	4.4
Sept	102.4	4.2
Oct	102.9	4.5
Nov	103.4	4.1
Dec	103.3	3.7
Jan	103.3	3.3

*13 January 1987 = 100

Table B Whole economy average earnings, seasonally adjusted

Month	Index (Jan 1980 = 100)	Percentage increase over 12 months	Estimated underlying percentage increase over 12 months
Sept 1986	187.1	6.1	7½
Oct	188.7	8.3	7½
Nov	190.2	8.1	7¾
Dec	191.3	7.4	7¾
Jan 1987	192.8	7.6	7½
Feb	191.2	7.4	7½
Mar	194.5	6.7	7½
Apr	195.9	6.4	7¾
May	198.1	8.7	7¾
June	200.0	7.7	7¾
July	203.1	8.1	7¾
Aug	201.6	7.6	7¾
Sept	201.4	7.9	7¾
Oct	203.4	8.0	8
Nov	207.3	8.5	8¼
Dec	210.1	8.6	8½

Chapter Nine
Conclusions

'The government then sent for the fire brigade, in the form not of an incomes policy (as in 1975) but of higher employment'. Clark and Layard, UK Unemployment (Heinemann Educational)

There are, as we have seen, many conflicting theories seeking to illuminate the causes and consequences of inflation and a similar number of policies aimed at controlling it. One of the few points of agreement seems to be that inflation is A Bad Thing – possibly The Worst Thing – and must be controlled at all costs. This agreement is surprising in view of the very weak theoretical justification for classifying inflation as a bad thing. Most of those who argue that it is indeed a bad thing seem implicitly to assume:

- some failure of the price mechanism, or
- that neglect leads to hyper inflations, or
- a regime of rigid exchange rates.

Economic theory and economic history are more equivocal on the issue. Some economists suggest that a moderate level of inflation is a positively good thing. It eases the task of the price mechanism and gently stimulates growth by ensuring adequate aggregate demand.

Even if the case for regarding inflation as a bad thing were to be accepted, this need not lead to a commitment to control inflation 'at all costs'. There may well be costs associated with inflation, but before embarking on a counter-inflation policy it is necessary to consider first how those costs compare with the 'costs' of possible cures.

Explanations of inflation (and the respective counter-inflation policies) fall into three broad groups – Keynesian, monetarist and cost-push. Keynesians argue that inflation occurs when aggregate demand exceeds the full-employment level of output and hence is an early indication that the government has followed a too expansionary fiscal policy. For Keynesians, then, controlling inflation means depressing aggregate demand and reducing the demand for labour. There is a clear connection here between the rate of inflation and the rate of unemployment, and this is apparent even after the famous breakdown of the Phillips curve (see for example Figure 16).

Conclusions

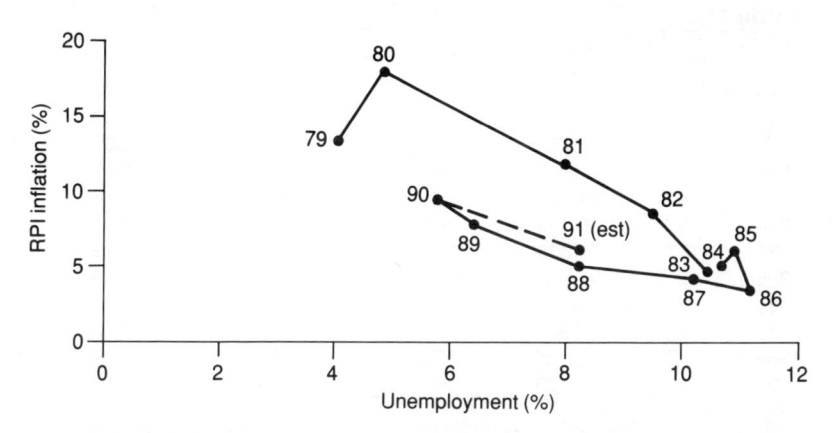

Figure 16 The inflation/unemployment trade-off

In Figure 16 we see that between 1980 and 1986 unemployment rose from 5 to 11 per cent, and this was accompanied by a fall in inflation from 18 to 4 per cent. Subsequently, as unemployment fell back to 6 per cent the rate of inflation rose to 10 per cent. This seems to be telling the Chancellor that one of the costs of reducing inflation is unemployment, and that having reduced inflation by imposing high unemployment it will revive as soon as employment revives – i.e. high unemployment is not a once-for-all cure but must be maintained into the longer term too.

Monetarists, on the other hand, claim that inflation results only and inevitably from an unmerited increase in money supply. The policy recommendations of the monetarists are therefore very clear – control money supply. This, provided expectations are speedily and rationally formed, is a simple, painless solution to the inflation problem.

Despite the clarity and simplicity of the message, mistakes have been made – and perhaps the best known is the 'Lawson boom' of 1988 (see Table 10). Inflation had been steadily reduced to 3.9 per cent in 1987, but there were signs that private sector credit could get out of control. Nigel Lawson cut both interest rates and income tax rates, and this spawned a huge increase in demand and a return to an upward trend in inflation. Inflation was back at 7.5 per cent by the end of the year and at 9.0 per cent by the end of 1990.

This inflationary expansion in demand (both fiscal and monetary) was neither intended nor, apparently, foreseen by the Chancellor, who subsequently (with the benefit of hindsight) admitted his mistake and he and his successor at the Treasury in October 1989 (John Major) followed a much tighter line – the famine after the feast.

UK inflation

Table 10

	Inflation* (%)	CGBR† (£b)	Bank Base Rate‡ (%)	Unemployment § (%)	Terms of trade
1980	18.4	11.158	17.0	6.8	103.8
1981	13.0	10.398	12.0	10.4	100.7
1982	12.0	7.855	13.0	12.1	99.2
1983	4.9	14.502	10.5	12.9	98.6
1984	5.1	10.165	9.0	13.1	97.4
1985	5.0	11.804	13.0	13.5/11.8	98.9
1986	5.5	8.460	11.5	11.7	96.8
1987	3.9	4.061	10.5	10.5	98.0
1988	7.5	−4.934	8.5	8.4	97.8
1989	7.7	−5.134	13.0	6.3	97.8
1990	9.0	−4.609	15.0	5.8	99.3

*Based on the RPI (all items), January to January; †Central Government Borrowing Requirement (−is surplus); ‡After Budgets; § Rebased in 1985

Sources: Christopher Johnson, *The Economy Under Mrs Thatcher 1970–1990*, Penguin, 1991; *Monthly Digest of Statistics* (various), HMSO

Mistakes aside, there were other problems with this simple painless remedy. The leading spokesman for the monetarists – Professor Milton Friedman – explicitly absolves the labour market from any blame in the inflation story. No-one and nothing can bring about inflation except the growth of money supply. There should be no need to impose any unemployment on the economy to lower the inflation rate.

Unfortunately, as the record shows, we have had the pain. Table 10 shows how high rates of unemployment preceded the decline in inflation rate, and as unemployment rate begins to fall inflation takes off again. The pain has been acknowledged as a price worth paying for low inflation. The practice and pronouncements of monetarists seem to belie the basic tenets of their faith.

The cost-push school of thought is rather more complicated than either the Keynesian or the monetarist. The focus here is switched to the income distribution aspects of the economy. Broadly there are four income groups in the economy – labour (which receives wages), capitalists (who receive interest), entrepreneurs (who receive profits) and rentiers (who receive rents). If rentiers – say in the form of OPEC – push up their incomes by raising rents, then in order to maintain total costs (and hence prices) the others must receive less. Labour may object to this fall in living standards and so push up their wages. Profits would then fall until entrepreneurs too rebelled and put up their prices to restore their profits. This can go on and on, around and around, with the ever-increasing spiral of costs and prices – the inflationary spiral.

'Being jobless is a price worth paying to beat inflation'

Chancellor Norman Lamont was at the centre of a political storm last night after he said the huge jump in unemployment was a "price worth paying" to bring down inflation.

The Opposition branded his remarks a disgrace, and said the Chancellor couldn't care less for the unemployed.

Mr Lamont told the Commons: "rising unemployment and the recession have been the price that we've had to pay to get inflation down."

When Labour MPs jeered and yelled at him the Chancellor shouted over their protests, and continued his speech.

He insisted: "that is a price well worth paying."

The remarks came just hours after a rise of 84,000 in the jobless total was announced by the government. The unemployment total went up for the 13th month in a row, and is now almost 2.2 million. Nearly 570,000 people have lost their jobs over the last year, as the recession has started, especially in the South.

Source: *Today*, 17 May 1991

This process may be sparked off by any income receiver provided they can exercise market power and push up their return beyond the free market level.

It is instructive, for example, to look at the rate of profit earned, in real terms (i.e. adjusted for inflation), by the non-oil part of the UK economy since 1970. This is shown in Figure 17.

The oil price hike in the mid-seventies clearly had a marked effect and halved the real profit rate from about 9 per cent to about 4.5 per cent. There was then a brief recovery before the second oil price hike of the late seventies brought the rate down to 2 per cent. However, since 1980, there has been a steady trend back up to 9 per cent again. Thus, whoever is going to lose out to OPEC it is unlikely to be the profit earners.

It makes sense in such a world to try to reduce the market power of factors of production so that these income disputes can be resolved via market mechanisms. Certainly the power of labour articulated through trades unions has been reduced under the monetarist regimes. This has been achieved partly directly through legislation, but partly too by imposing high levels of unemployment which greatly weakens the will of those in work to risk their jobs for greater rewards.

To some extent the recession (whether contrived or accidental) will not only weaken trades unions but will also put pressure on entrepreneurs not to increase their prices. Many businesses are working below capacity or even going into receivership, and this is the capitalist's equivalent to unemployment of labour.

One of the factors in the cost-push theory is the relative price of our imports over our exports. This is called our *terms of trade*, and Table 10 shows how they moved in our favour from 1980 to 1986 and there-

UK inflation

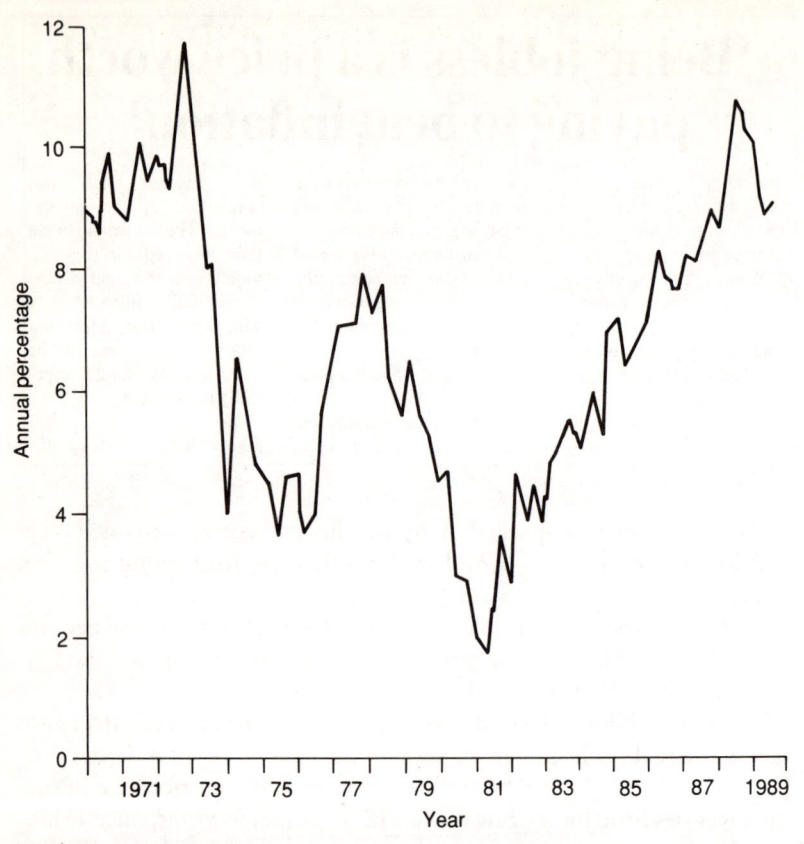

Figure 17 Company profitability – real rate of return for non-North Sea industrial and commercial companies (Bank of England figures)

after turned against us. Some economists have therefore argued that the inflation rate in the UK is primarily determined by our terms of trade rather than anything our government can influence.

If this theory has anything at all to commend it, then the only way to counter inflation is to resolve the income distribution issue first. This seems to call for a national council of some kind in which the various groups could 'carve up the national cake'. This would be anathema to free-marketeers, but without perfectly competitive, perfectly operating markets, the market mechanism is simply not up to the job.

Reading list

'Economy in transition', *Lloyds Bank Economic Bulletin*, Dec. 1991.
Layard, R., 'Pay leap-frogging', *Economic Review*, Nov 1991.

Conclusions

One of their own number, or not

A statistician, say the facetious, is somebody who is good with numbers but does not have the personality to be an accountant. The next director of the Central Statistical Office after Sir Jack Hibbert retires next February will need more than personality. For the poor quality of Britain's economic statistics makes steering the economy like driving a car with steamed-up windows, wonky dials and no lights.

When the government advertised the job in July, it outraged the statistics profession by saying that applicants did not need to be professional statisticians. The government's in-house number-crunchers, already demoralised by hefty spending cuts in their department during the 1980s and a dwindling public confidence in their figures, have taken this as a further snub.

Within the professional lifetime of the CSO's top men Britain once boasted the best economic statistics in the world; now *The Economists*'s good statistics guide ranks it ninth out of ten countries. In Britain, GDP stands more aptly for grossly deceptive product, and RPI for ropey price indicator.

Source: *The Economist*, 7 September 1991

Index

Aggregate
    demand 42, 46
    supply 42, 46
Announcement effects 68
Banham (John) 60
Bank credit 76
Barber boom 43
Basket of goods 10
Cartels 55
Cash (*see Money*)
Cheques (*see Money*)
Cobweb model 67
Common currency 80
Communist countries 4
Company profitability 88
Consumer confidence index 62, 63
Consumers' expenditure deflator 19
Core inflation 20
Cost of living index 12
Credit controls 72
Creeping inflation 7
Demand 42, 46
Exchange rate
    fixed 24, 25
    floating 24, 25, 78
    mechanism (ERM) 68, 79
Expectations 62
    Phillips curve 50, 62, 78
    regressive 63
    rational 66
Family expenditure survey 13
Fiscal drag 27
Fiscal policy 44, 80
Fisher equation 34, 58
Fixed exchange rate 24, 25
Flexible prices 3
Floating exchange rate 24, 25, 78
Friedman 32, 73, 81, 86
Galloping inflation 7
Gaps
    inflationary 44
    deflationary 44
Godley (Wynne) 37, 43
Gold standard 36, 44

Goodhart's Law 78
Gradualism 66
Greenbacks 35
Hanson (Charles) 16
Headline inflation 18
Heath (Edward) 22
Howe (Sir Geoffrey) 74
Hyperinflation 7
International Monetary Fund (IMF) 72, 78
Index
    consumer confidence 62, 63
    cost of living 12
    retail price 12
    taxes and prices 17
    wholesale price 19
Indexation 17
Income distribution 23, 57, 86
Inflation
    core 20
    creeping 7
    galloping 7
    headline 18
    hyper 7
    price 48
    pure 6
    severe 7
    underlying 18
    wage 47
    year on year 7, 16
Inflationary gap 44
Interest rate policy 76
Keynes 40, 47, 62
Labour productivity 48, 61
Lawson (Nigel) 70, 79, 80, 81
    boom 43, 85
Layard (Richard) 61
Legal tender (*see Money*)
Lewis (Stephen) 41
Major (John) 2, 8
Market power 55
Medium of exchange (*see Money*)
Menu costs 24
Mild inflation 27

Money
- bank credit 76
- cash 73
- cheques 73
- legal tender 73
- medium of exchange 40
- M0 34, 73
- M3 76
- £M3 74
- M4 34, 74
- M5 74, 76
- PSL1 74, 76
- PSL2 74, 76
- quantity of 32
- quantity theory 33
- store of value 40

Monopoly power 56
Medium term financial strategy (MTFS) 68, 74
Natural rate of unemployment 50, 65
Non-accelerating rate of unemployment (NAIRU) 50, 64, 65
Organisation of petroleum exporting countries (OPEC) 17, 55, 57, 86
Pensions 23
Phillips curve 47, 58, 64, 70
- breakdown 49, 84
- expectations augmented 50, 78
- labour productivity 48, 61
- vertical 51

Prices
- flexible 3
- relative 5
- retail 12
- wholesale 19

Prices and incomes policies 70
Productivity 48, 61
Profitability 88
Public sector borrowing requirement (PSBR) 74
Public sector liquidity (PSL1, PSL2) (*see Money*)
Purchasing power of the pound 5, 16
Pure inflation 6
Quantity theory of money 33
- Cambridge equation 34
- Fisher equation 34, 58

Rational expectations 66
Real unit labour costs 26
Regressive expectations 62, 63
Retail price index (RPI) 12
Ridley (Nicholas) 37
Severe inflation 7
Shoe leather costs 24
Stagflation 49, 58
Store of value (*see Money*)
Social contract 71
Taxes and prices index 17
Terms of trade 87
Thatcher (Margaret) 73, 80
There is no alternative (TINA) 68
Trades unions 56
Underlying inflation 18
'U' turns 68
Value added tax (VAT) 17
Velocity of circulation 33, 50
Vertical Phillips curve 51
Walters (Sir Alan) 80
Wage differentials 57
Wage inflation 47
Warburton (Peter) 43
Wealth distribution 23
Wholesale price index 19
Wilson (Harold) 71
Year on year inflation 16, 17